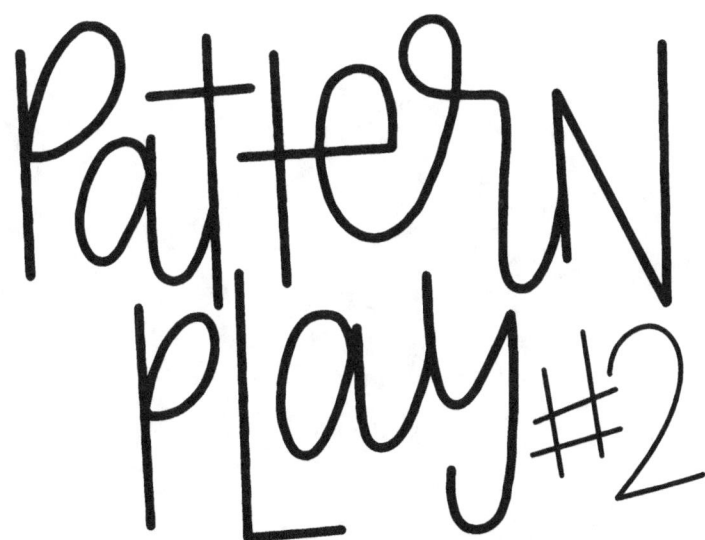

COLORING BOOK

**by Tara Larson Nearents
of Rad And Happy**

WWW.RADANDHAPPY.COM

Pattern Play Coloring Book
©2016 Rad And Happy
Huntington Beach, CA 92648

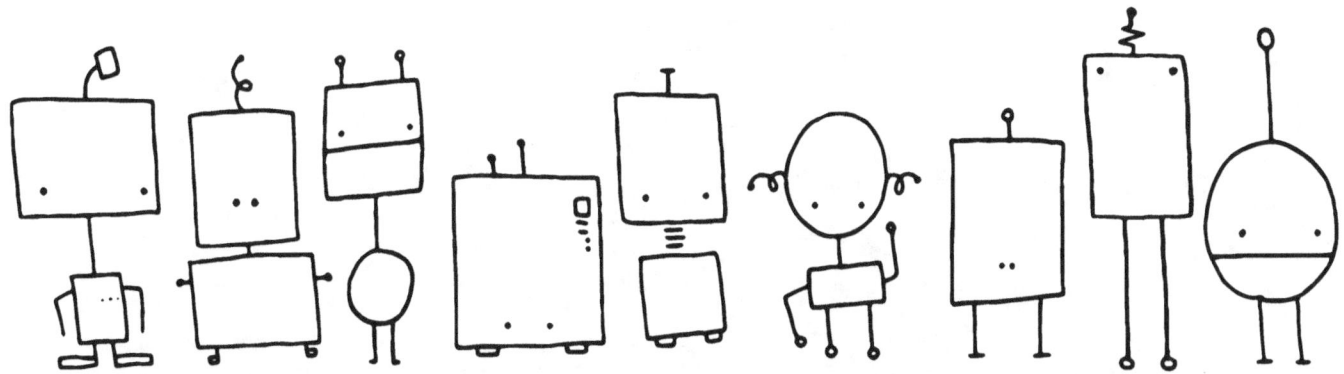

USE THIS PAGE TO TEST MATERIALS

Hey you.. Feel free to spread the love on social media
via @radandhappy and #radandhappycoloring
to possibly have your work featured and connect with
other insanely talented coloring masters like yourself.

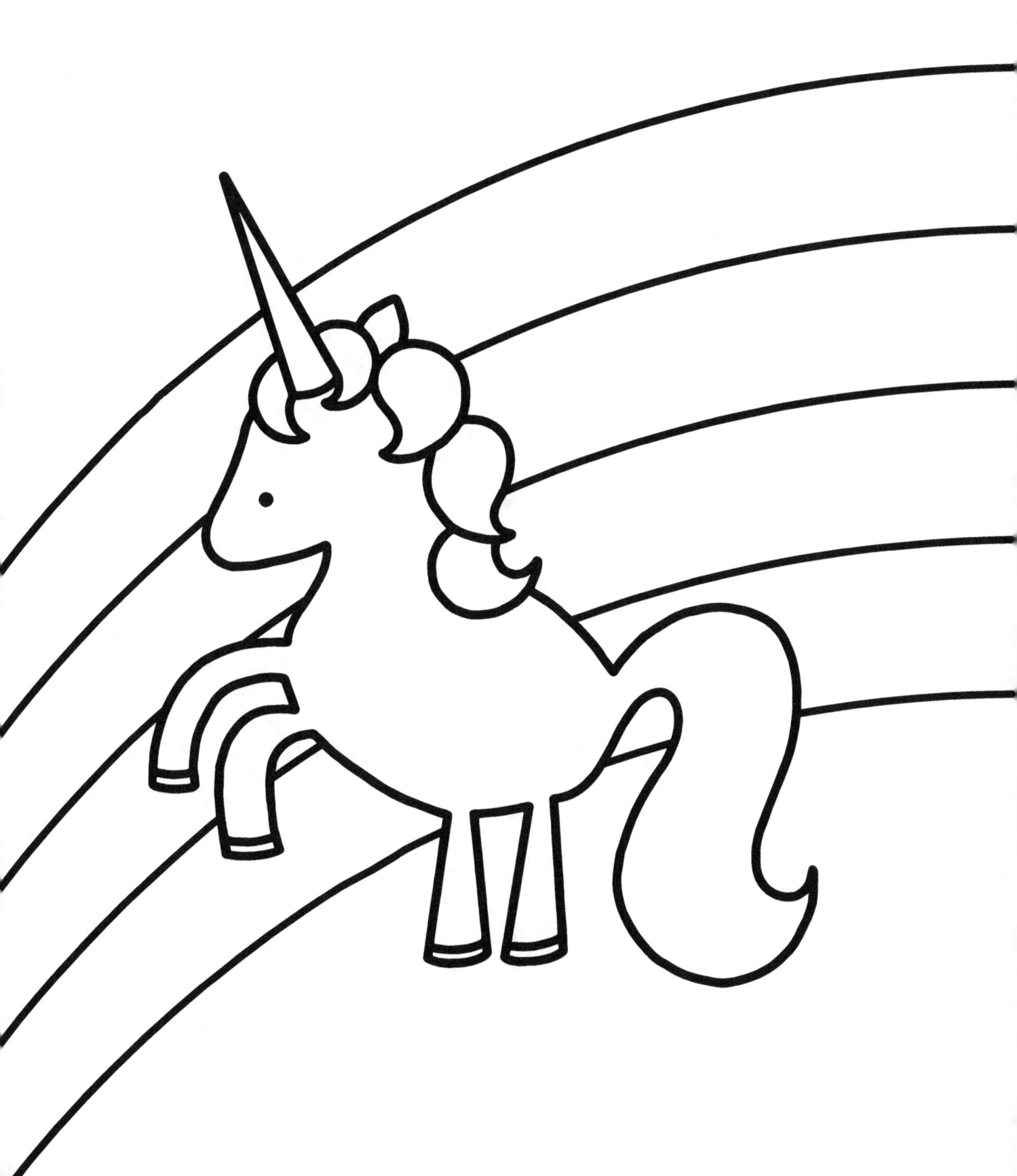

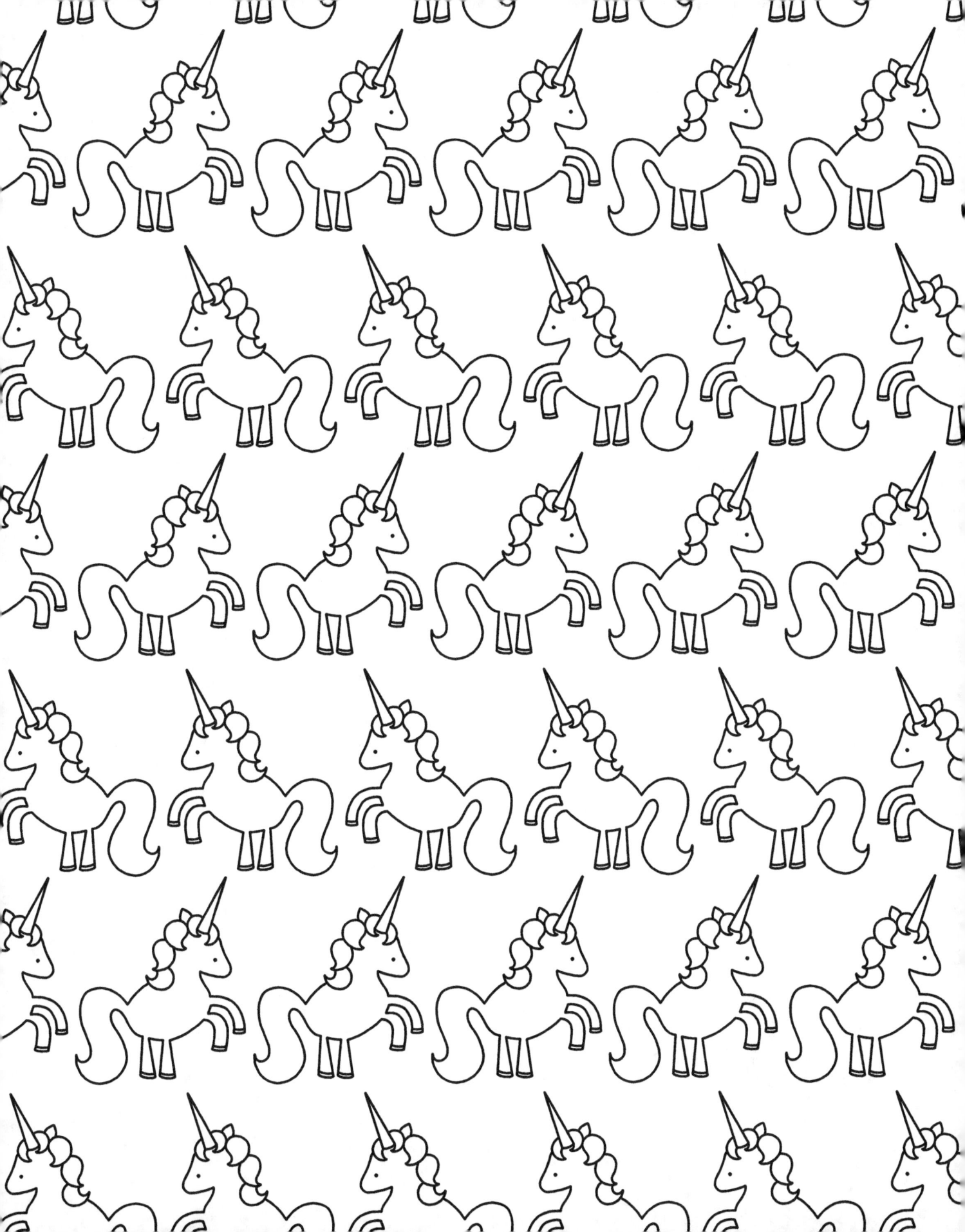

HEY THERE GOOD LOOKIN'

LOVE LOVE
LOVE LOVE
LOVE LOVE

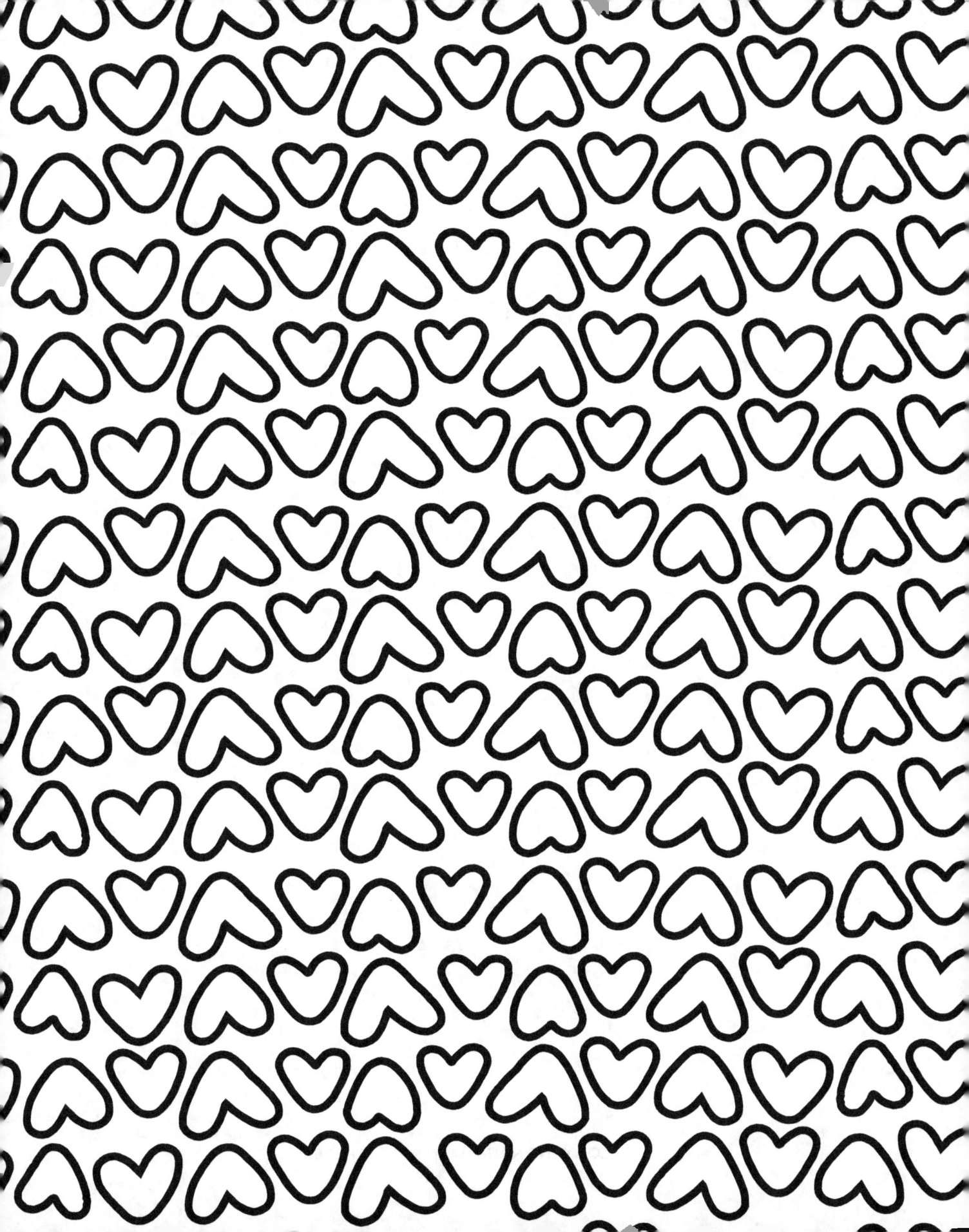

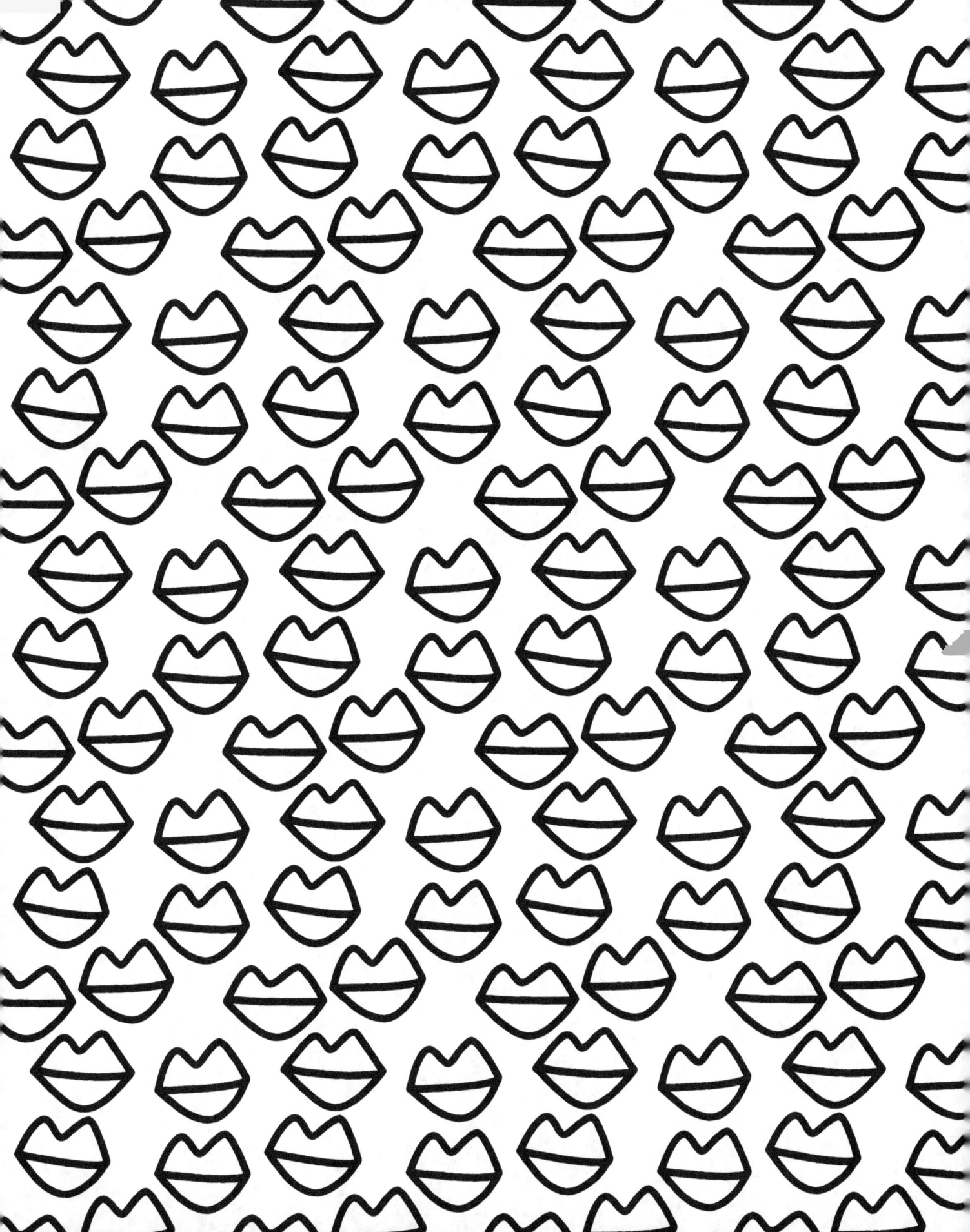

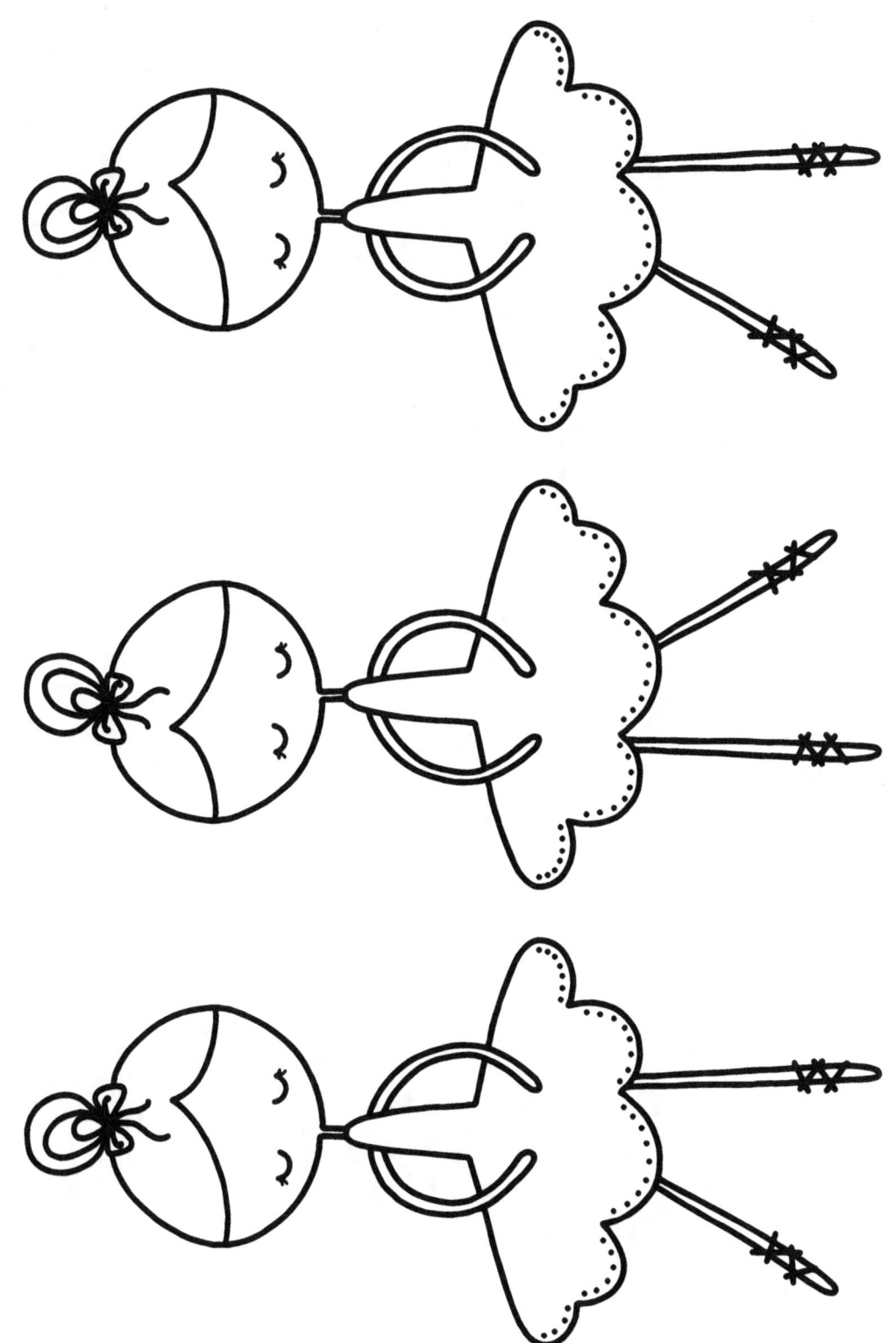

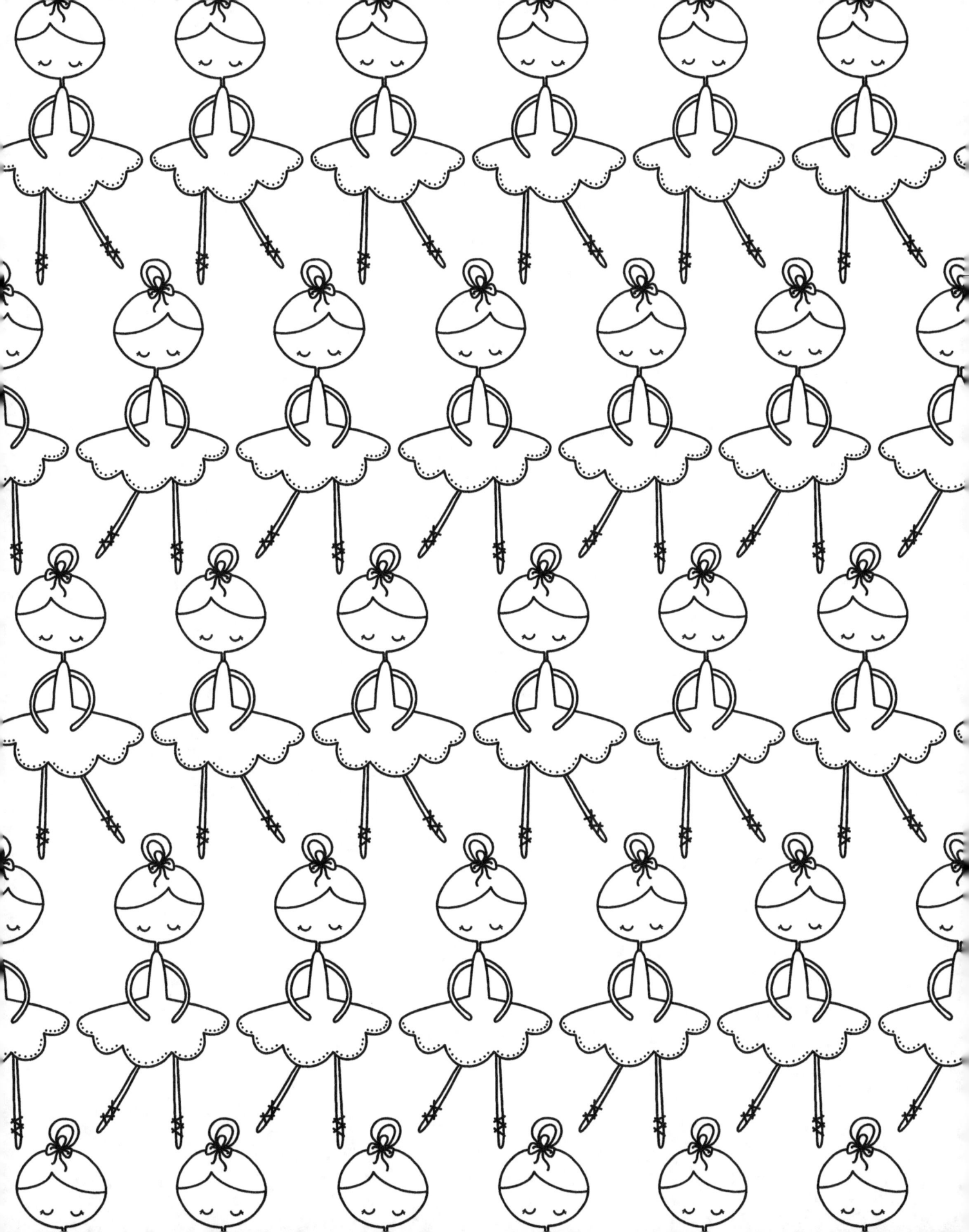

Let's Flamingle

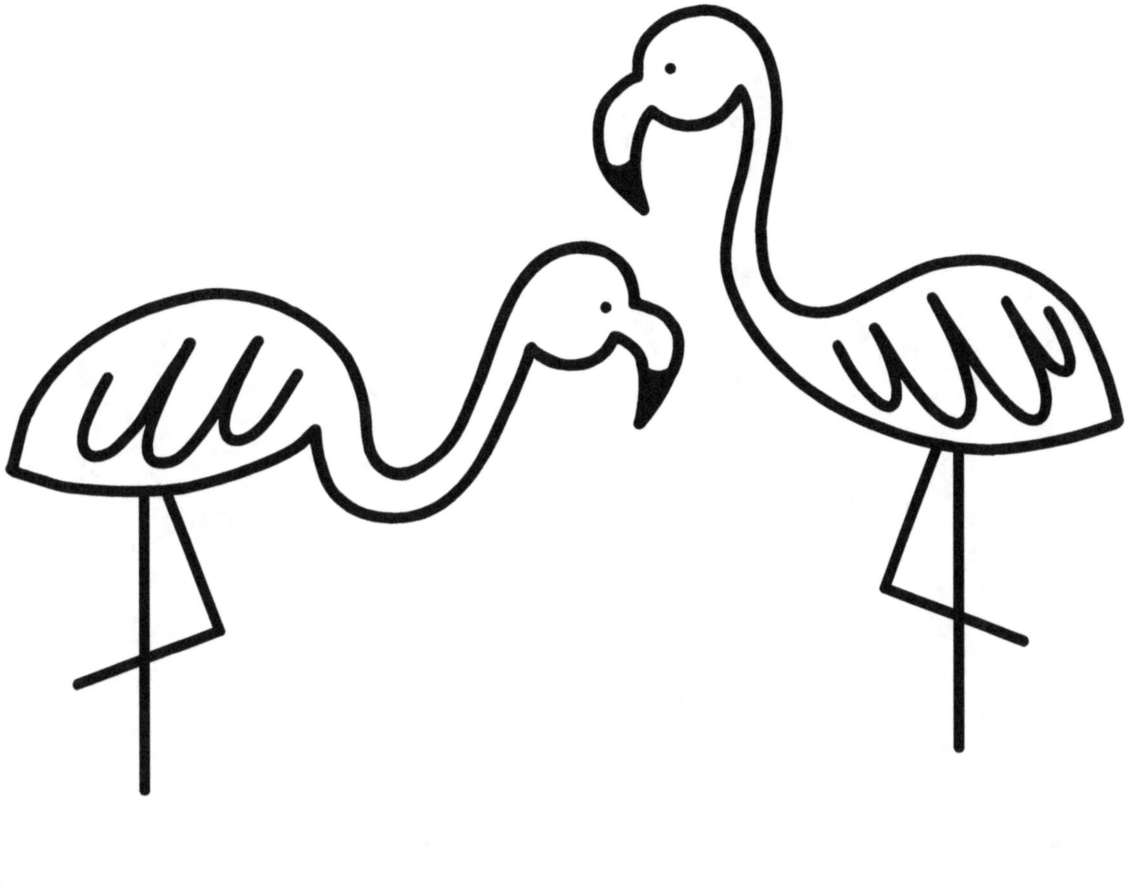

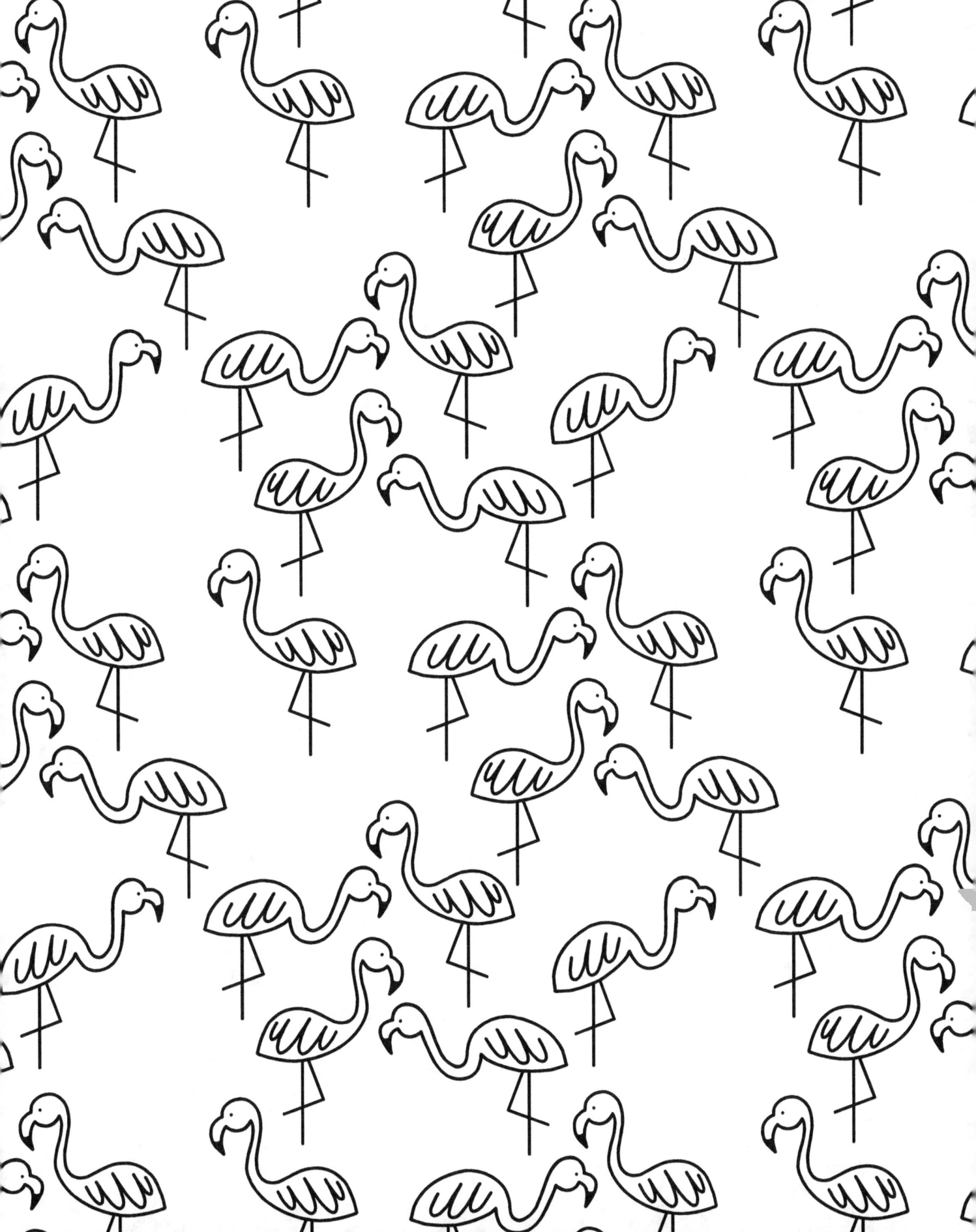

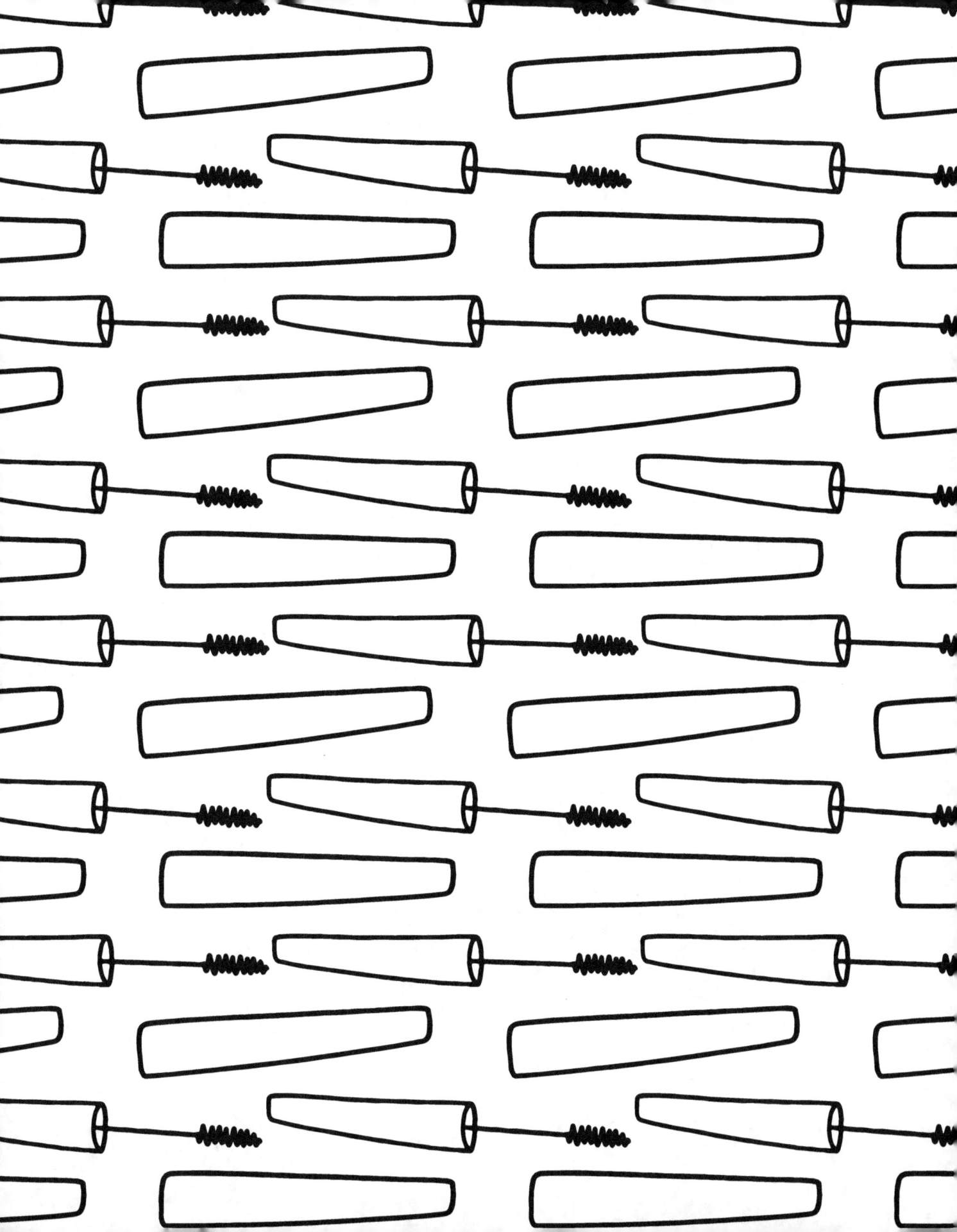

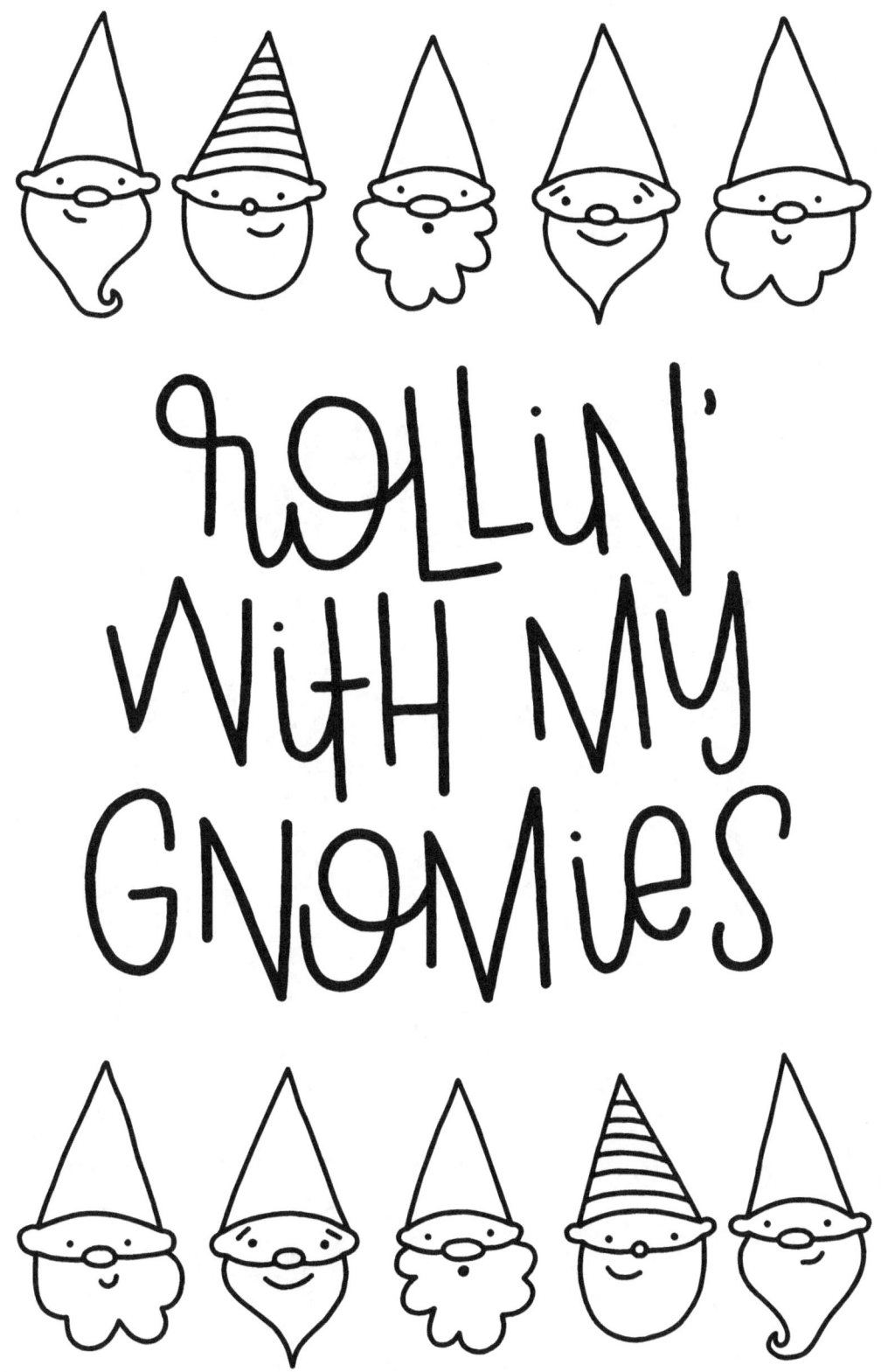

YOU ARE BETTER THAN SPRINKLES AND UNICORNS COMBINED

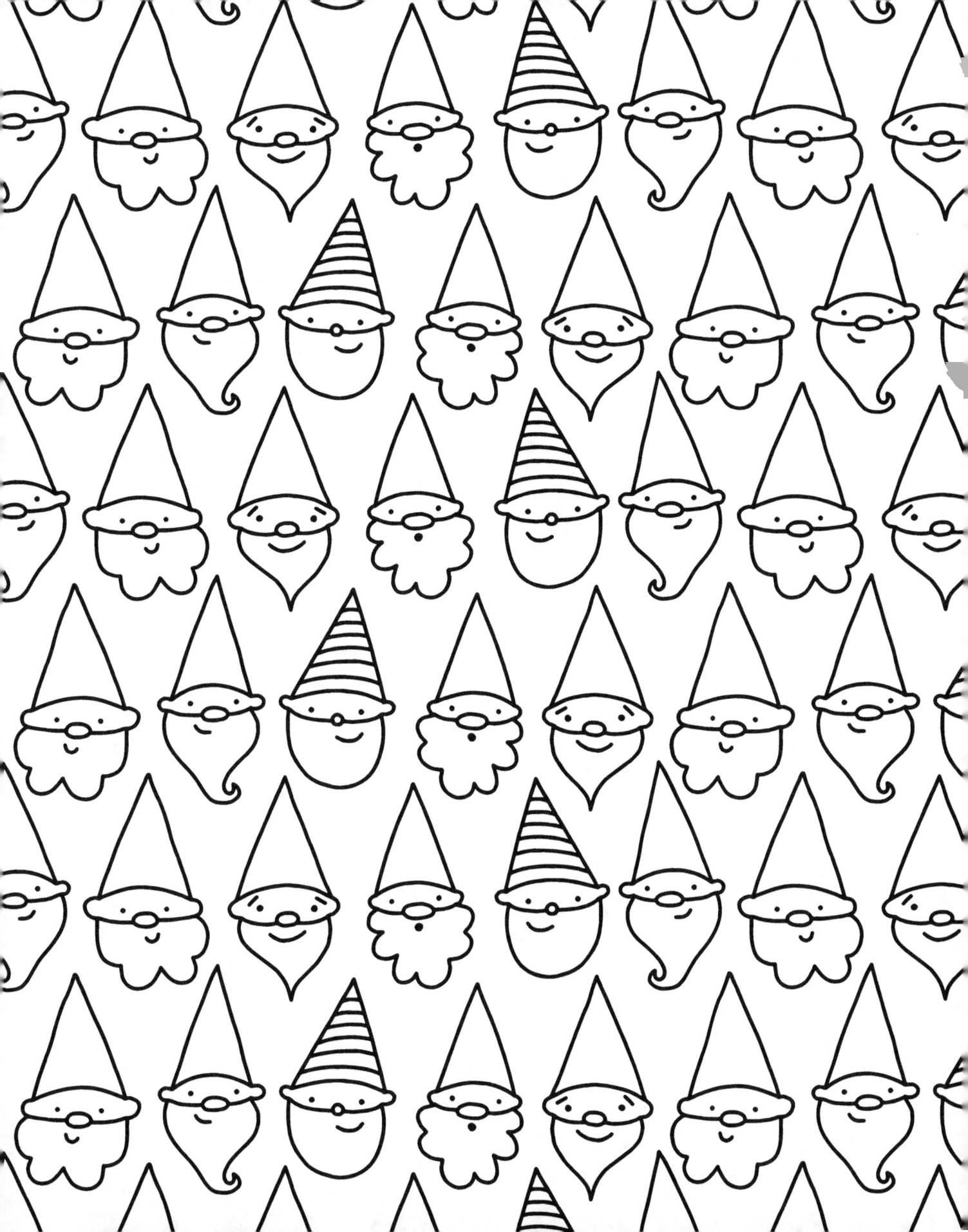

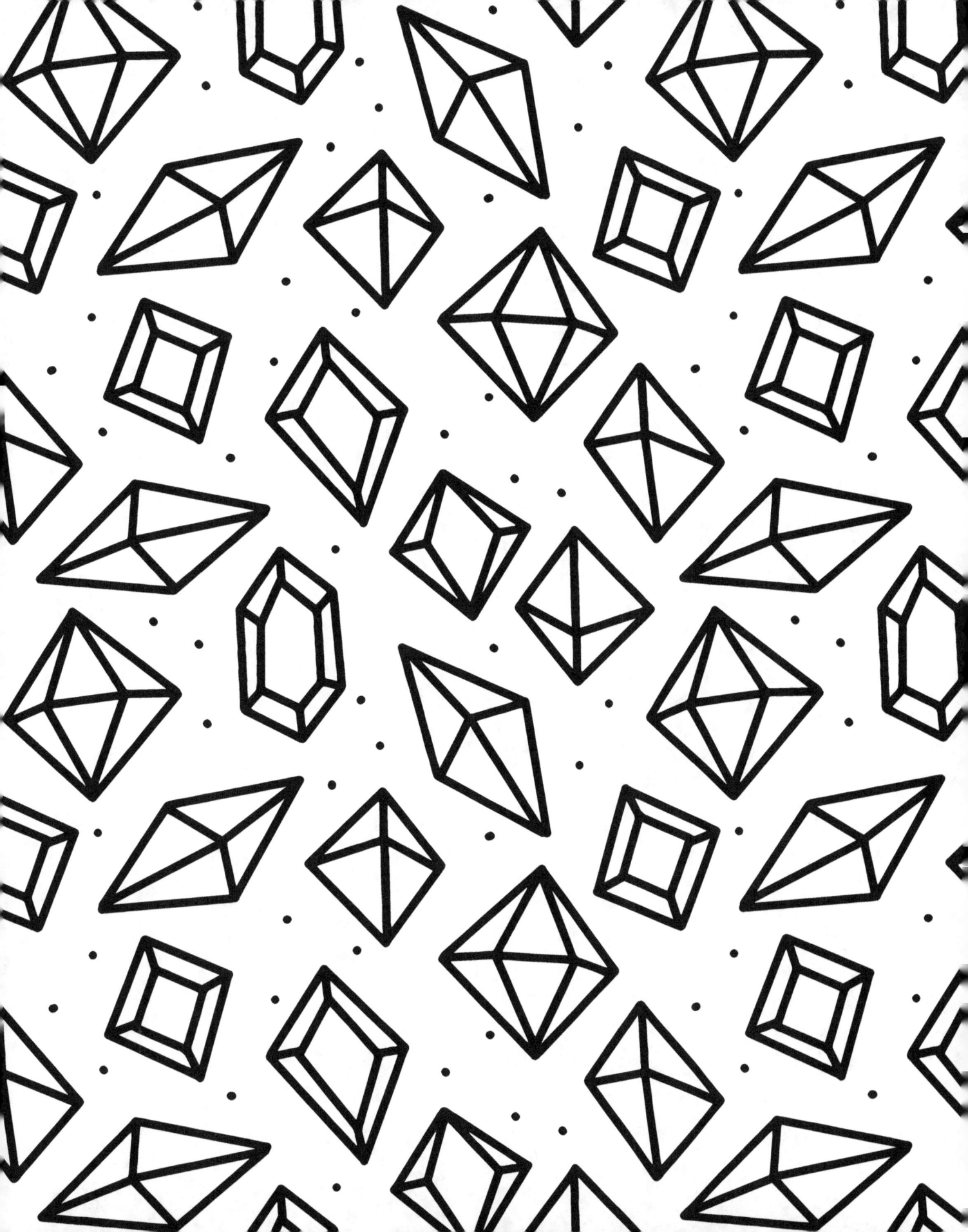

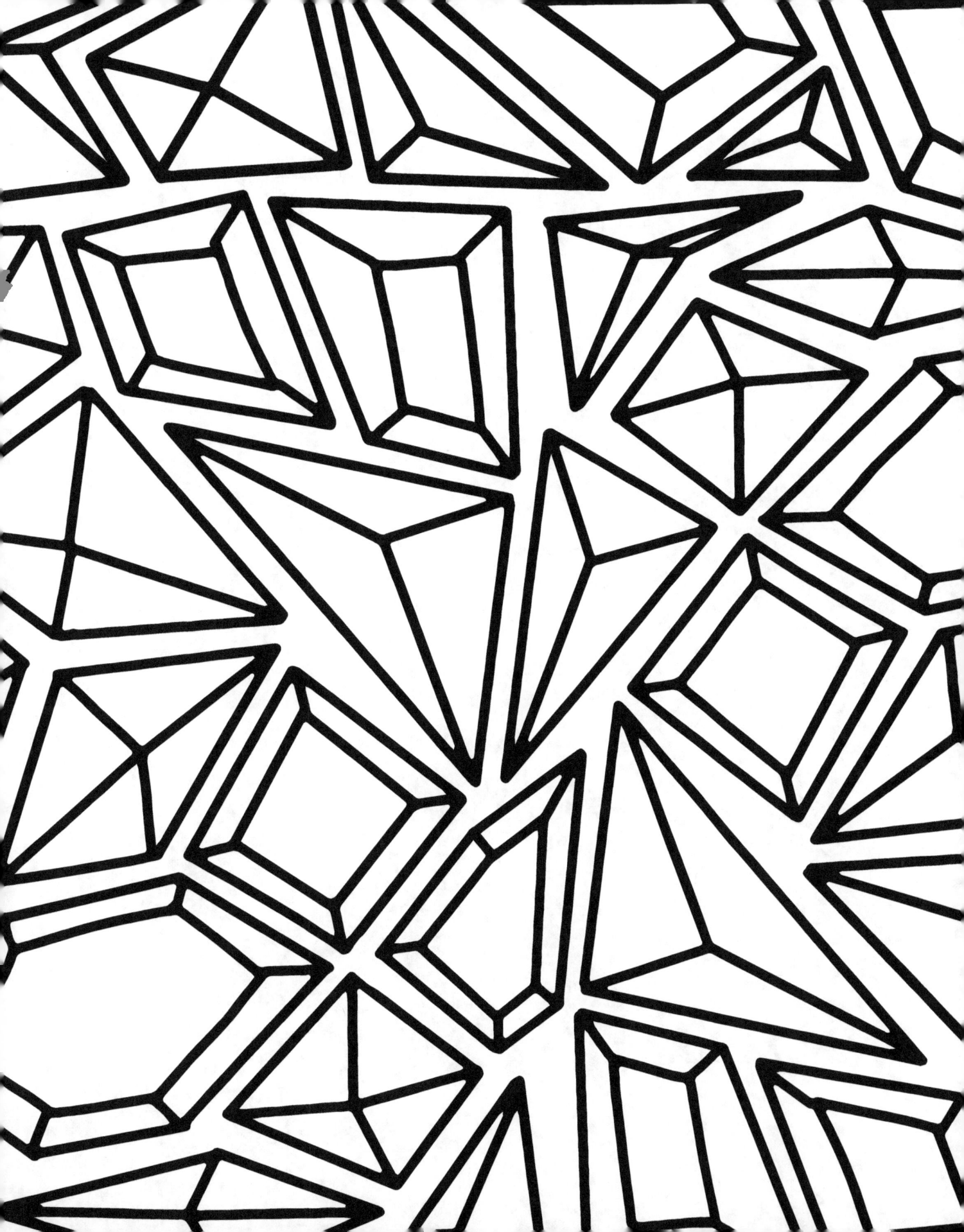

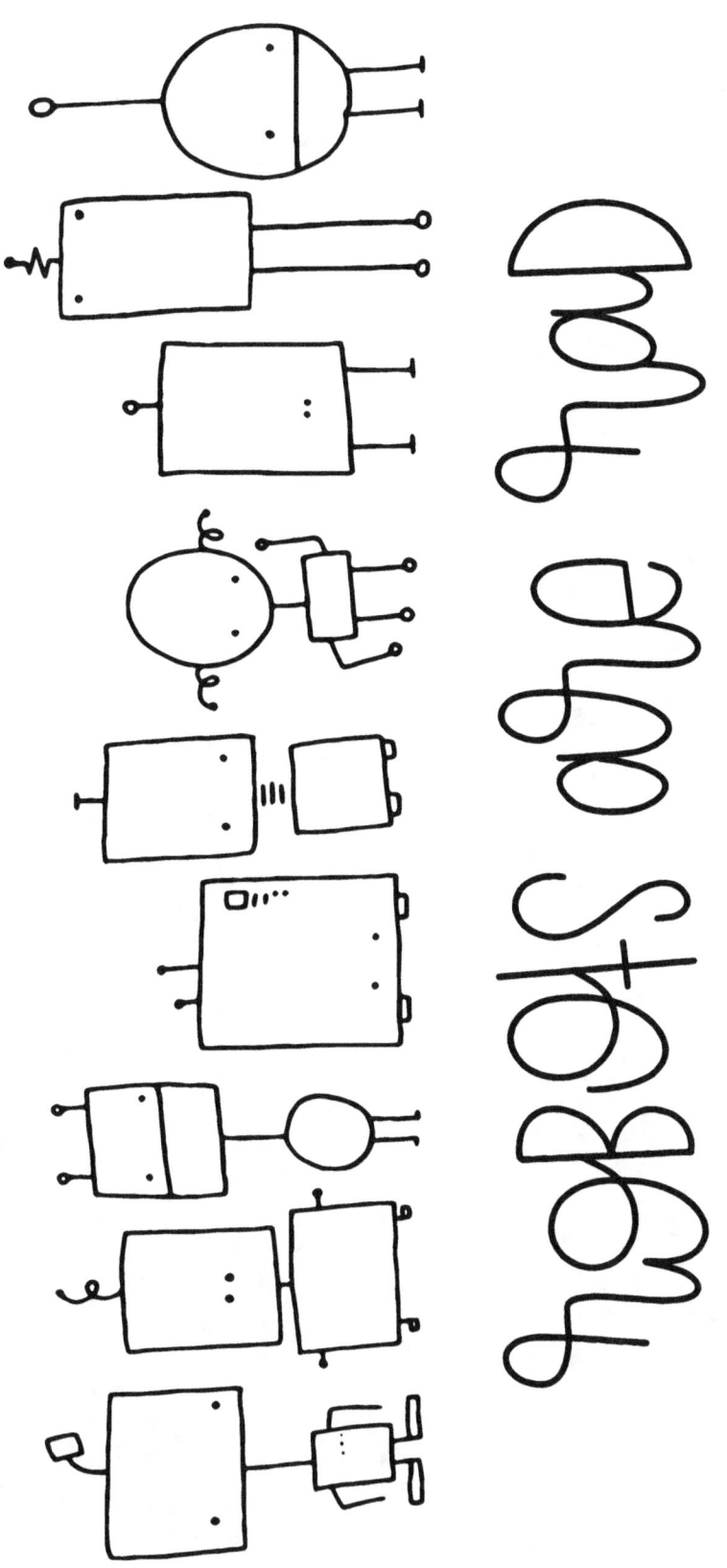

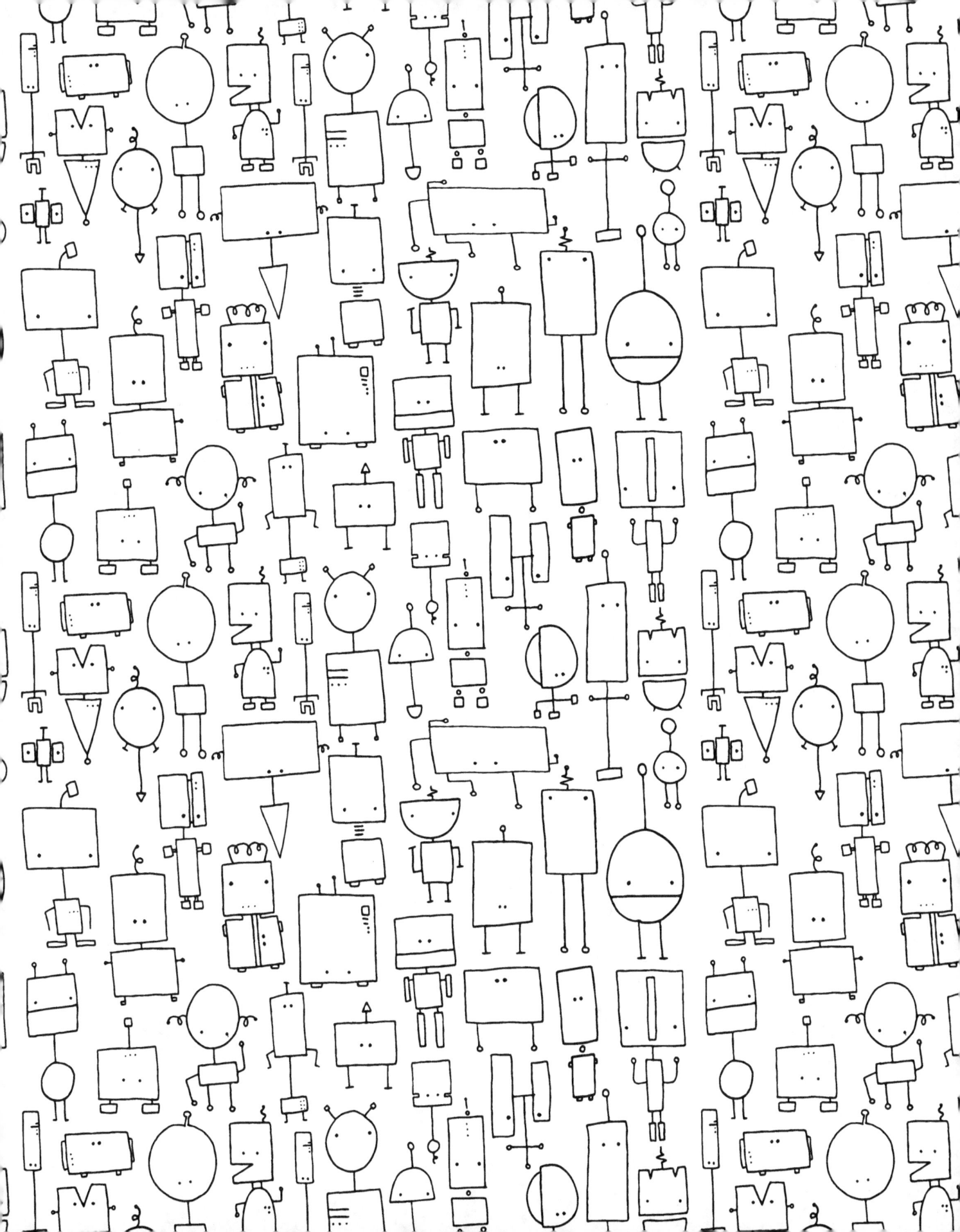

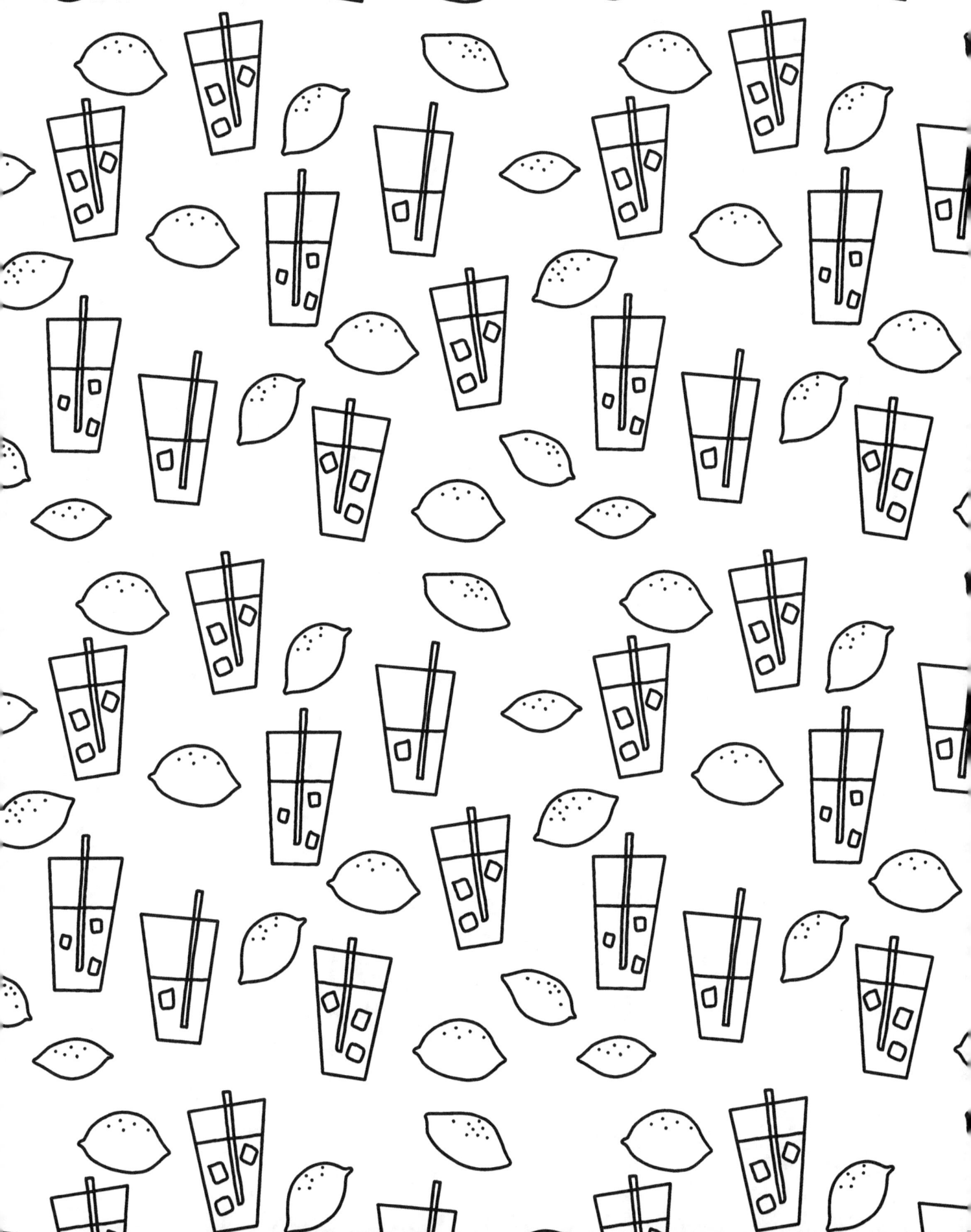

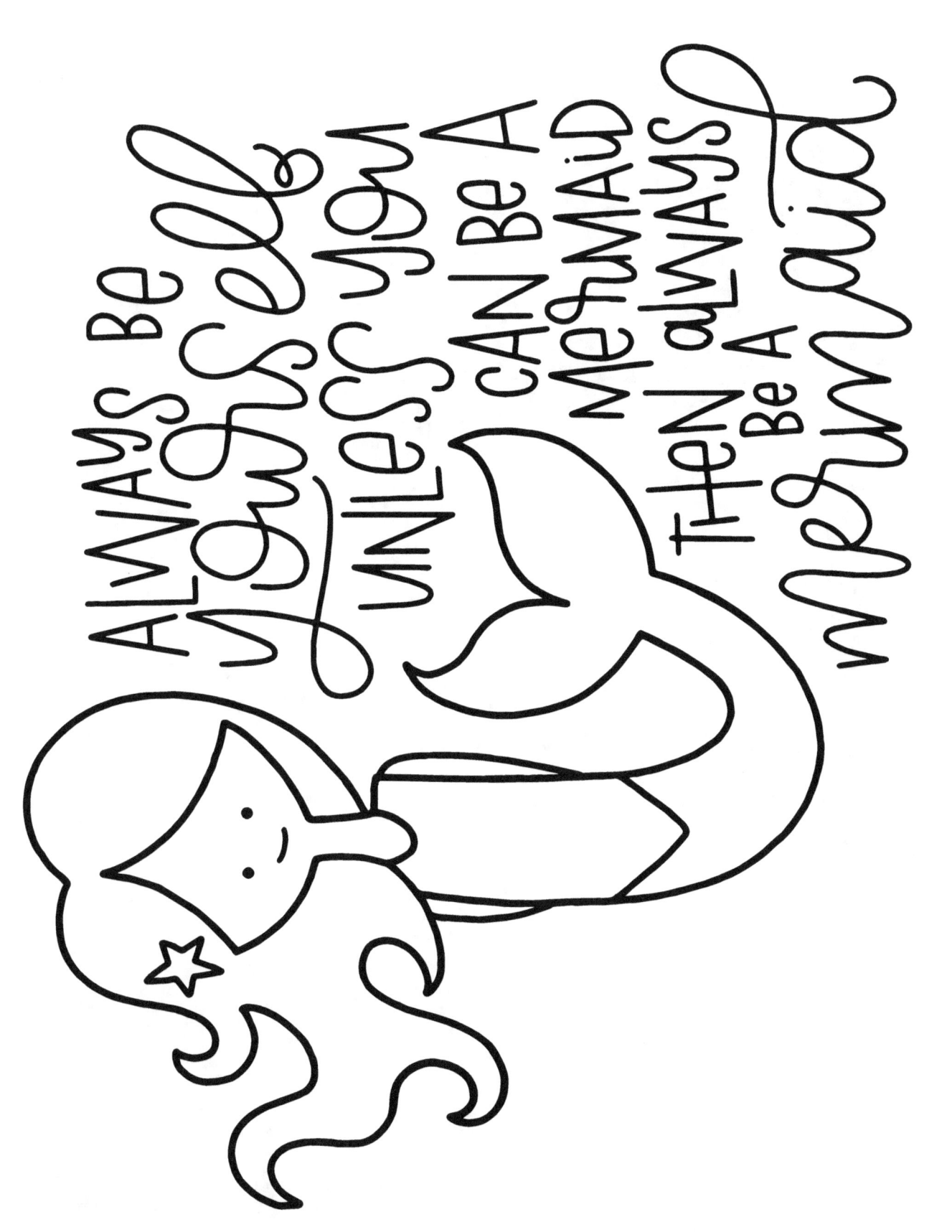

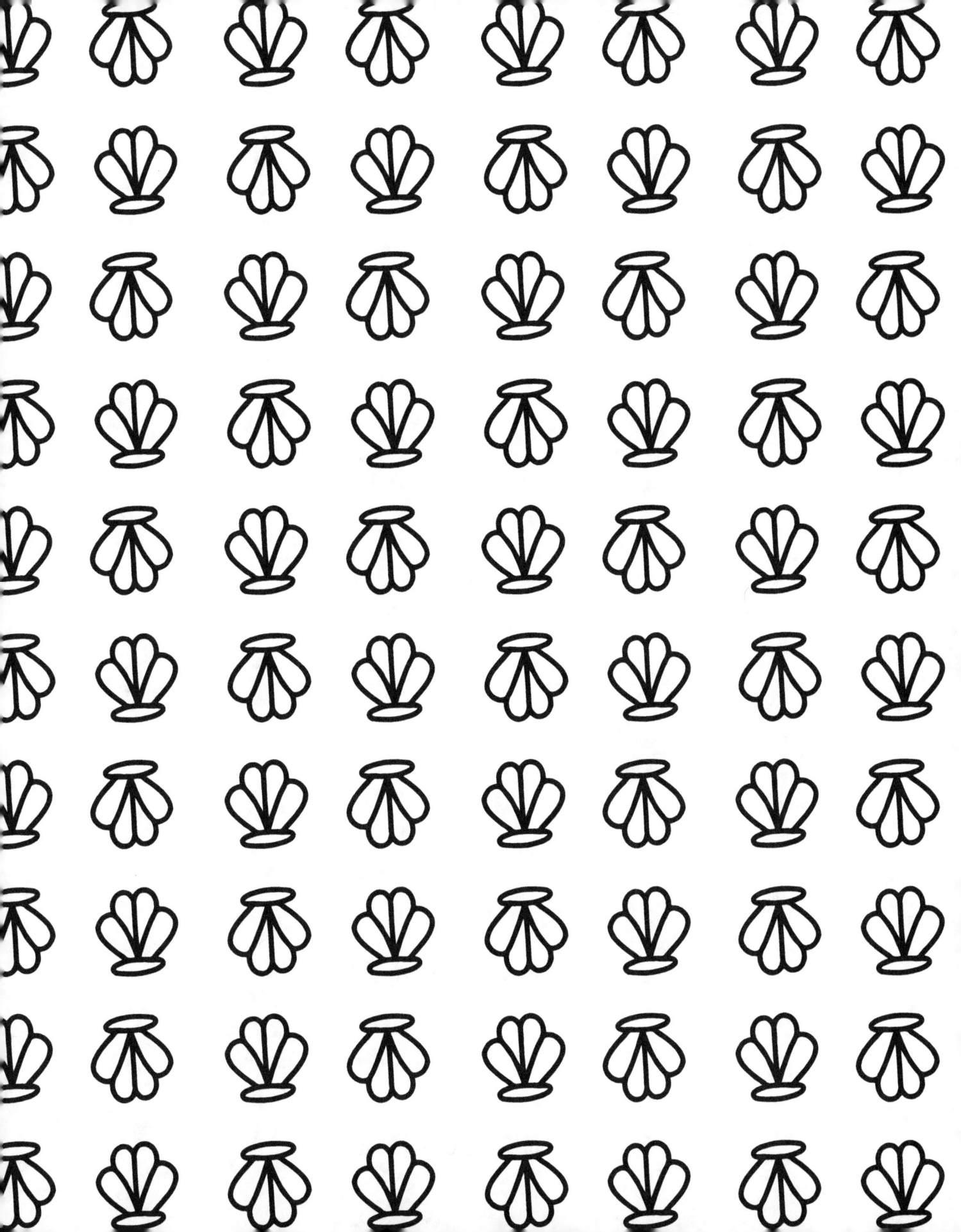

YOUR SKILLS ARE MAGICAL

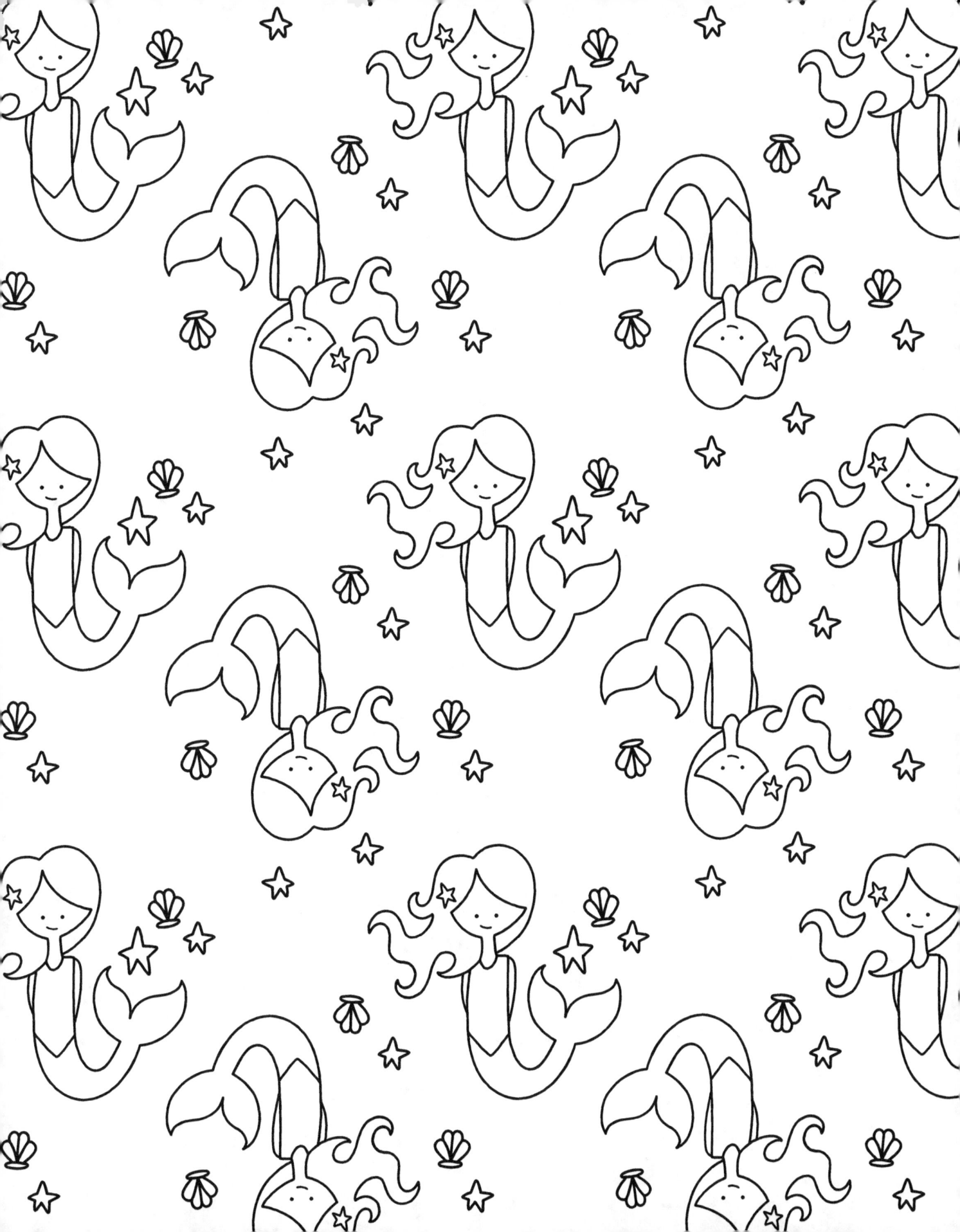

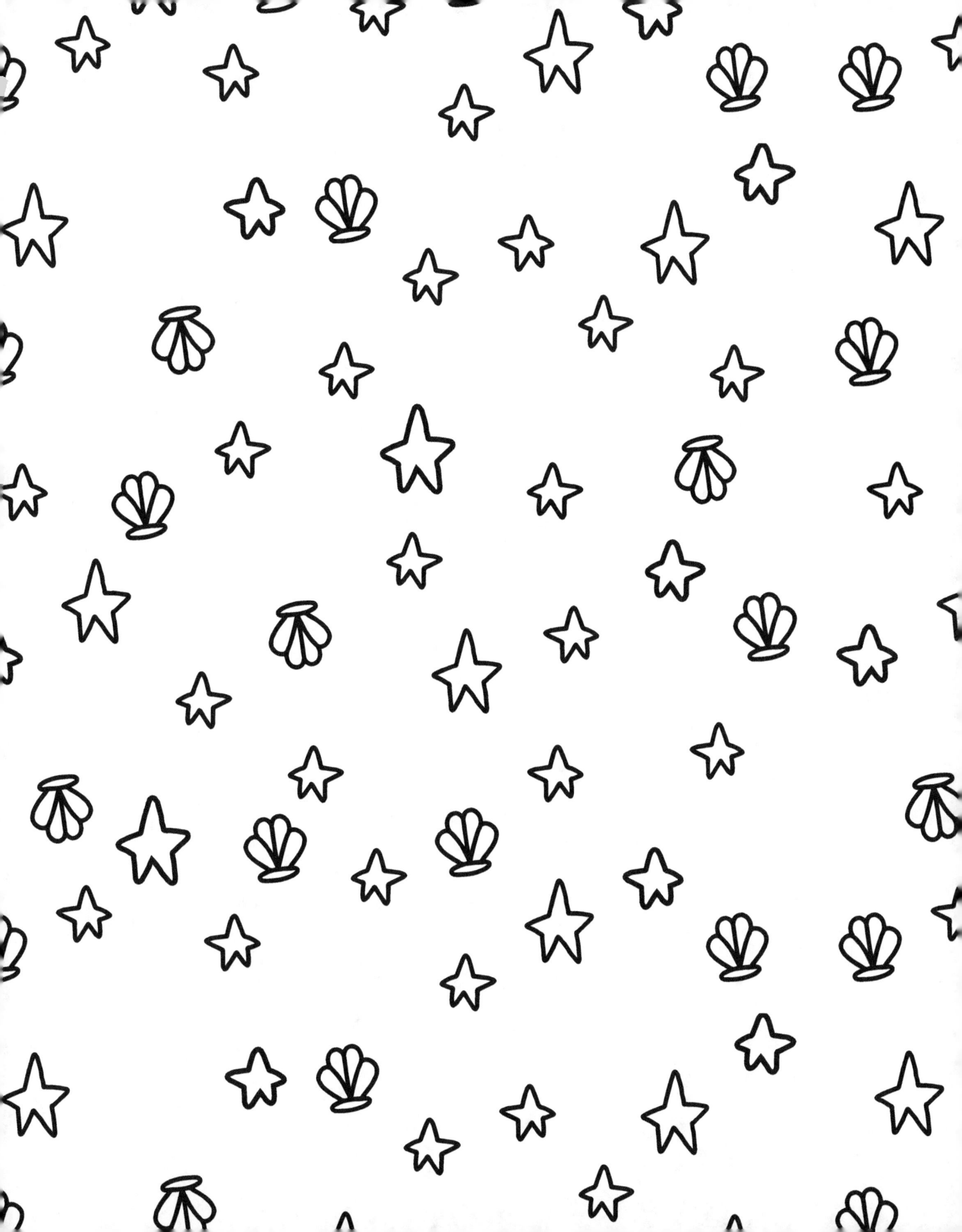

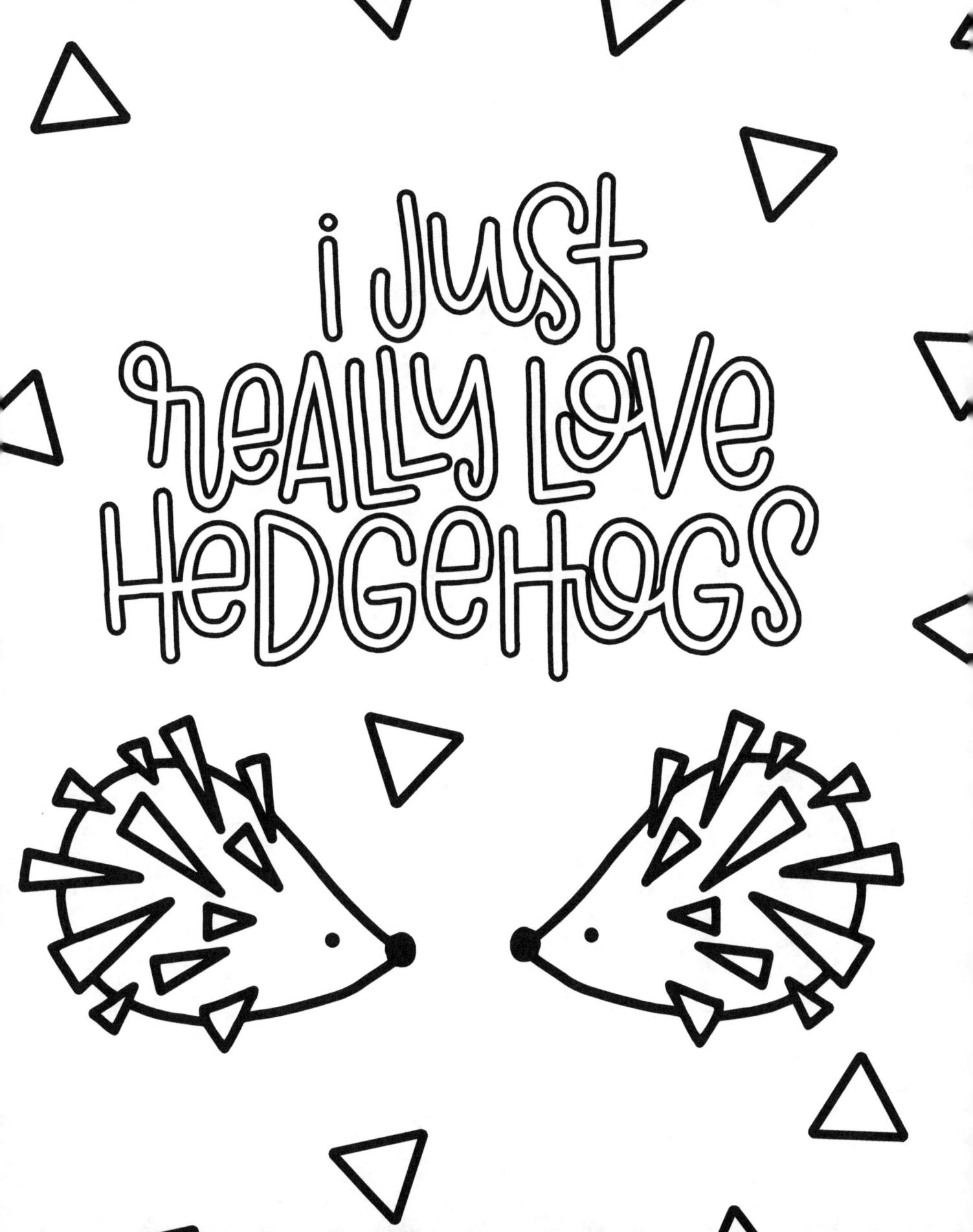

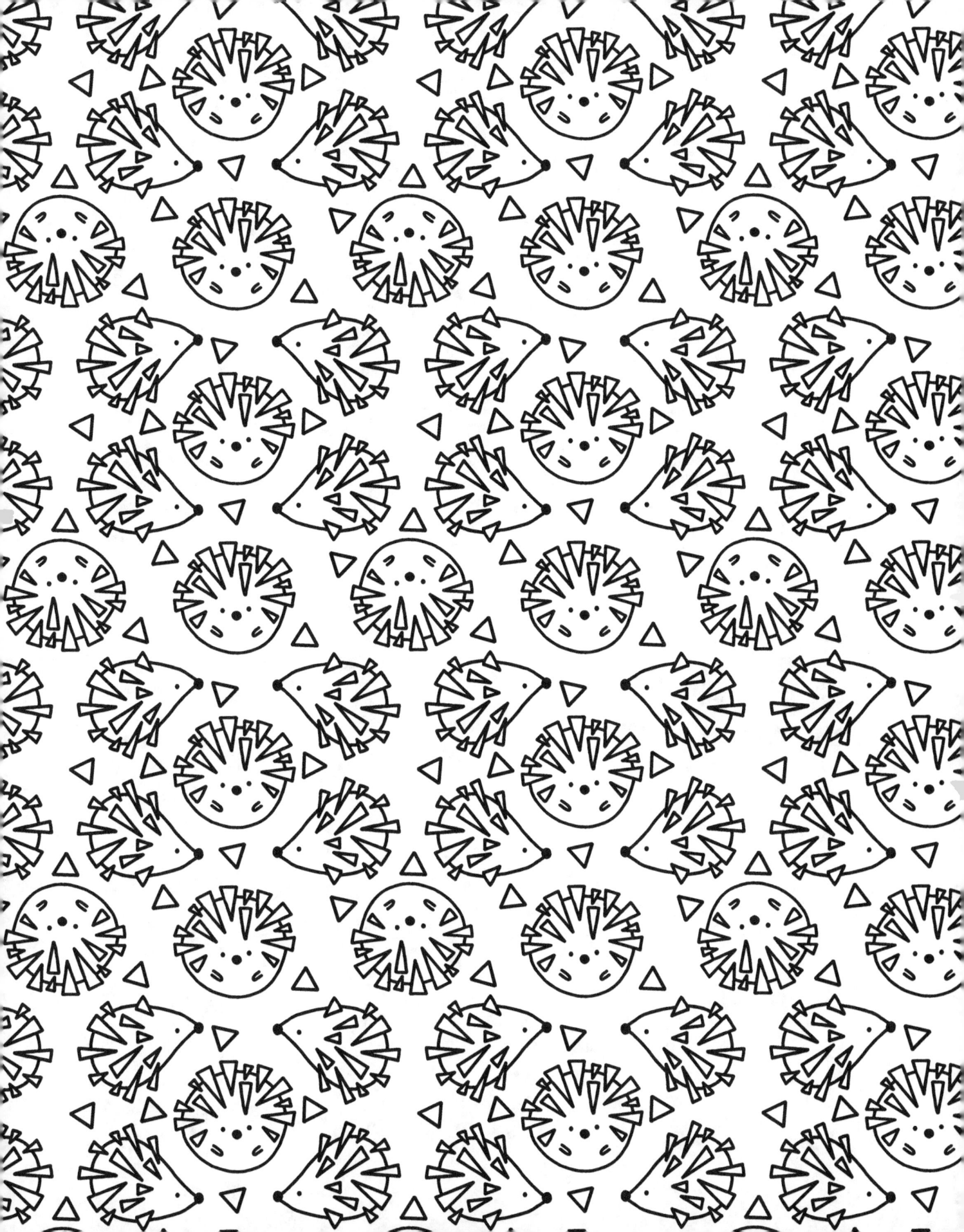

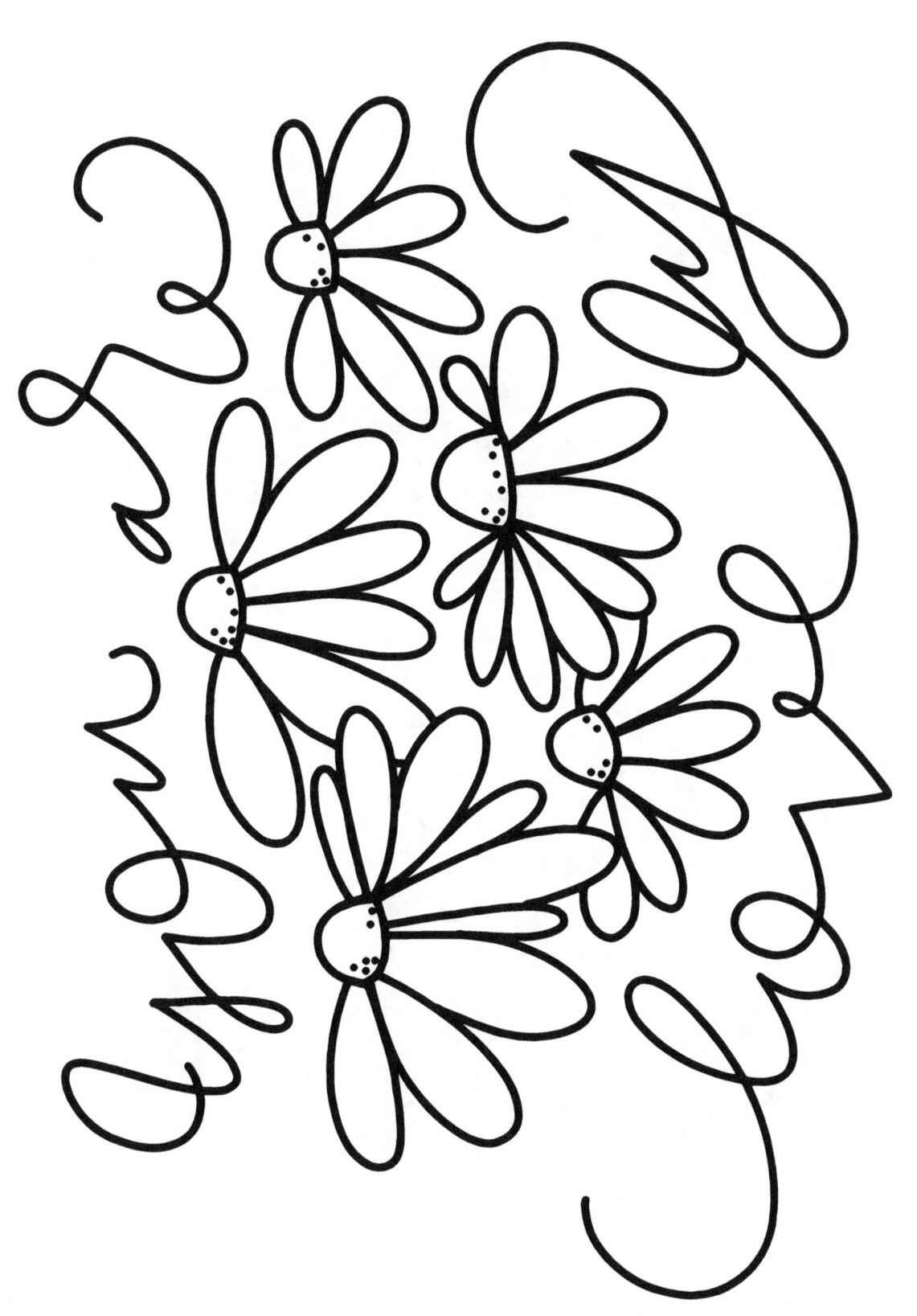

YOUR SKILLS INSPIRE ME

HOW ARE YOU SO DANG TALENTED?

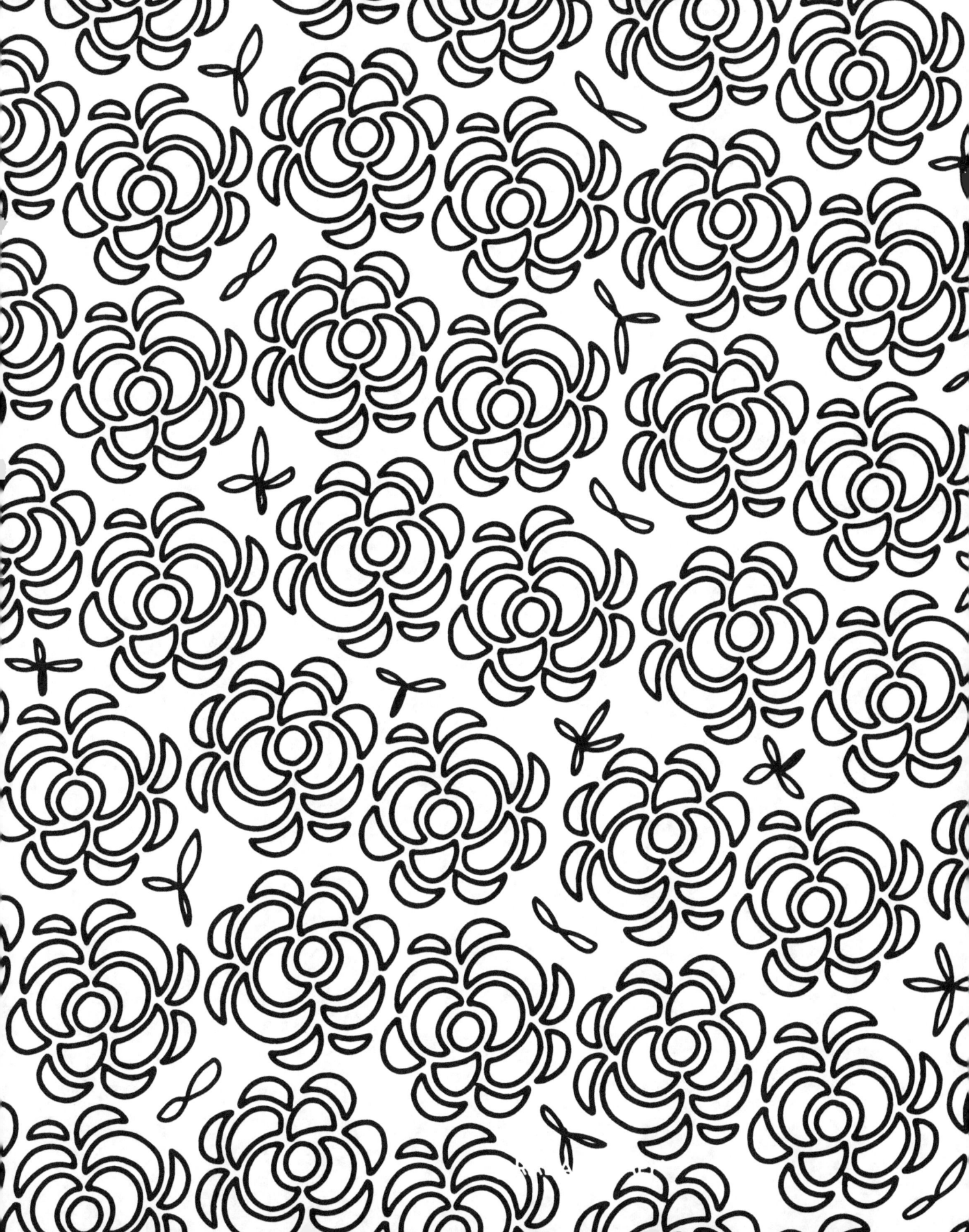

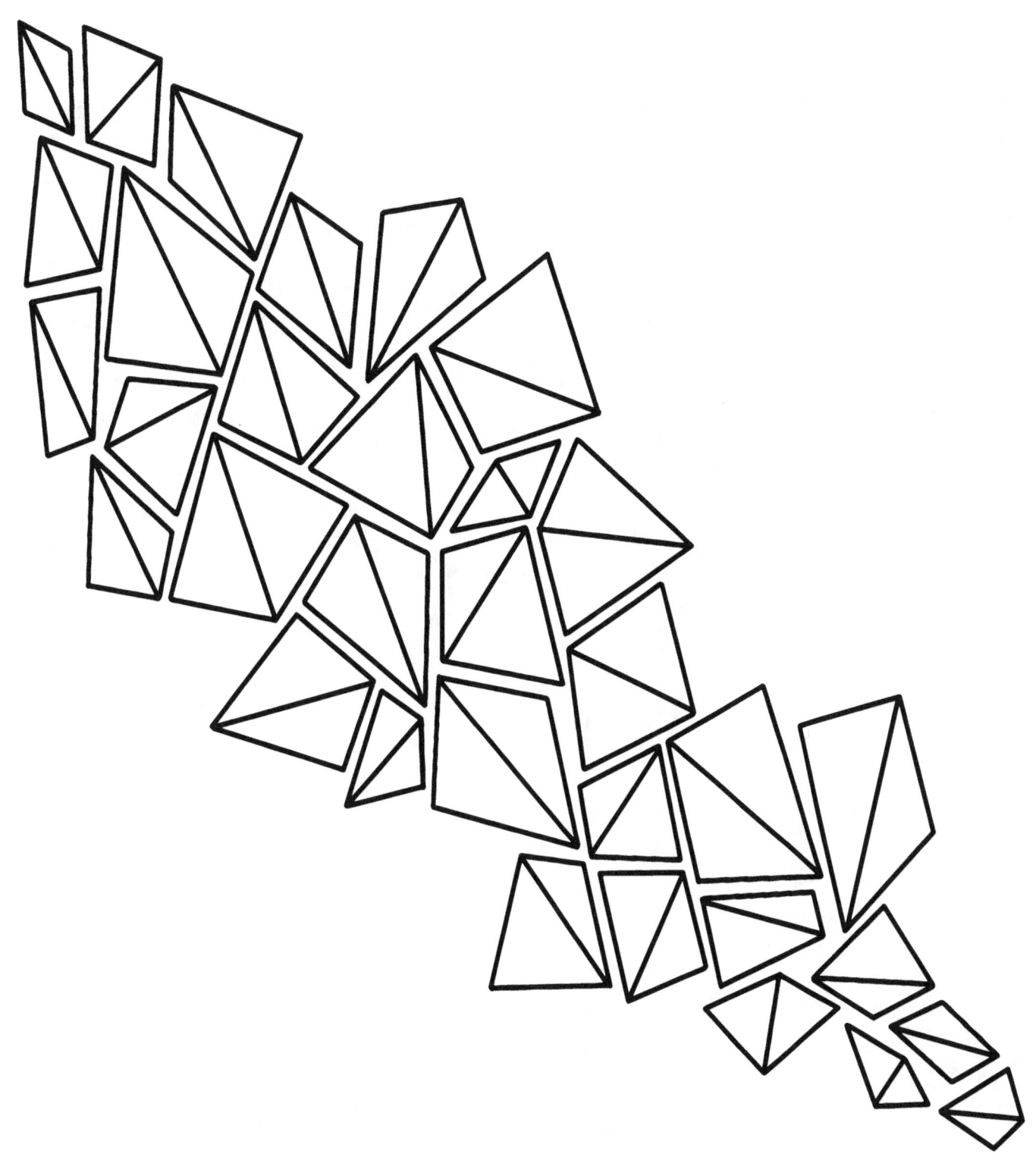

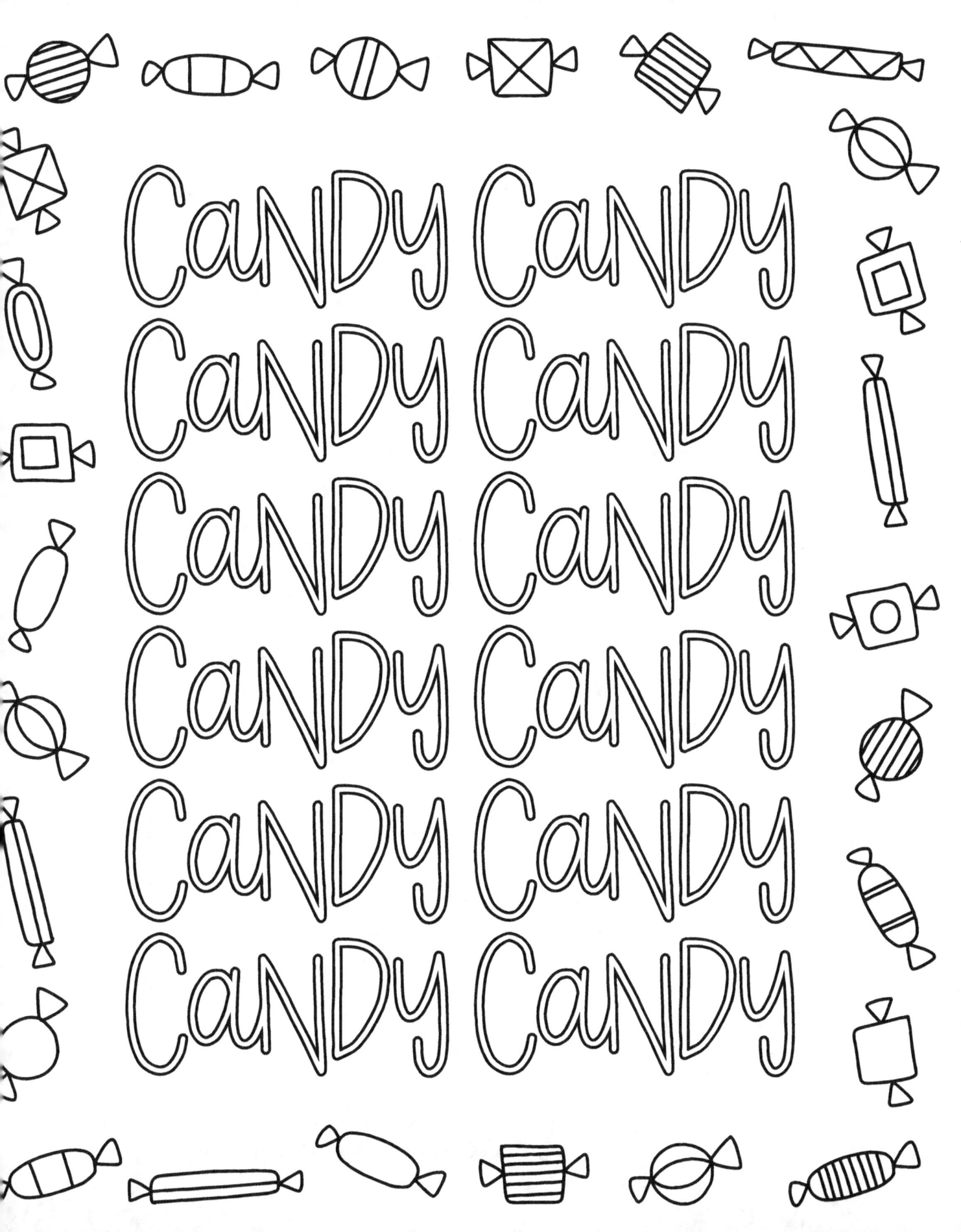

TWO THUMBS UP MY FRIEND

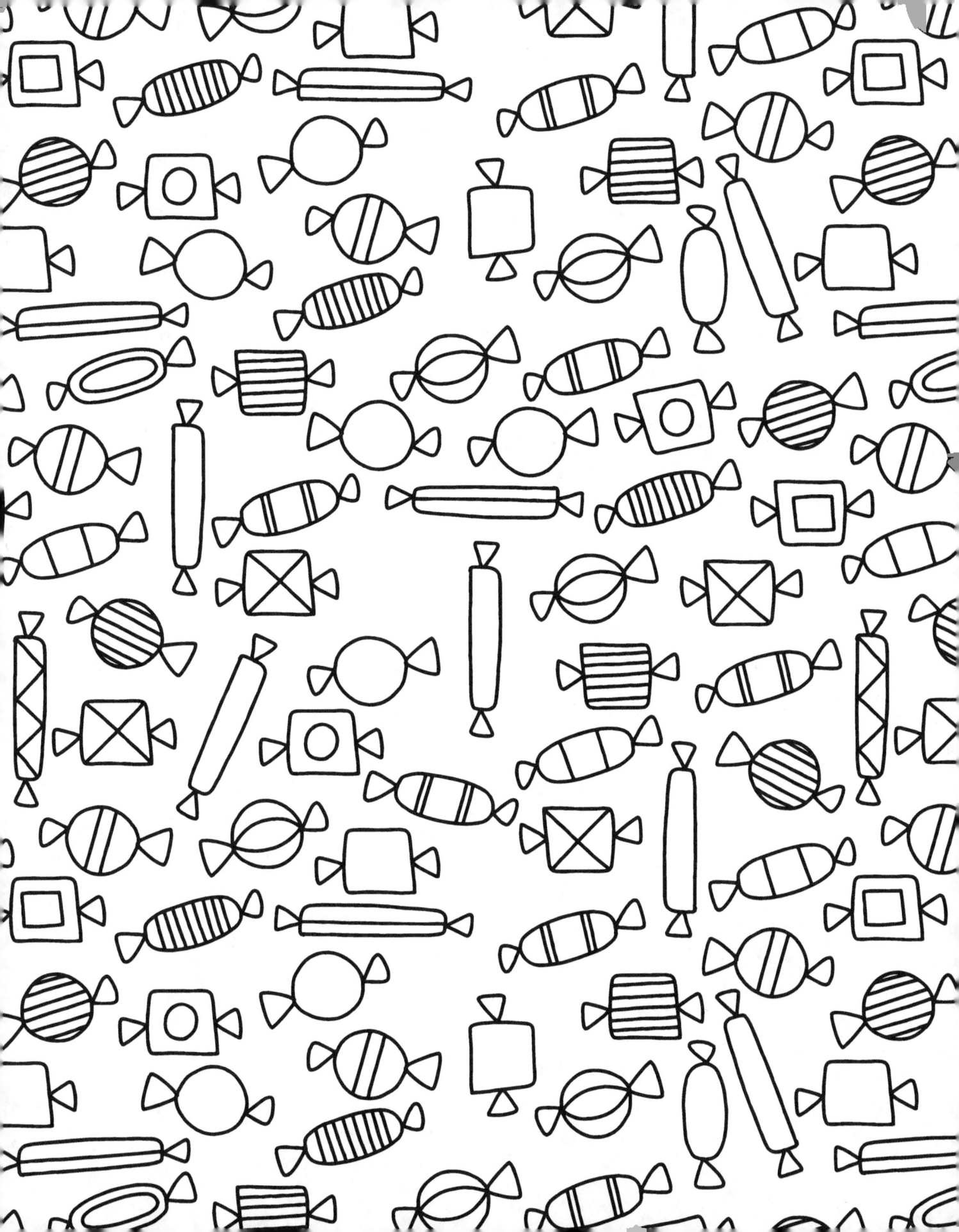

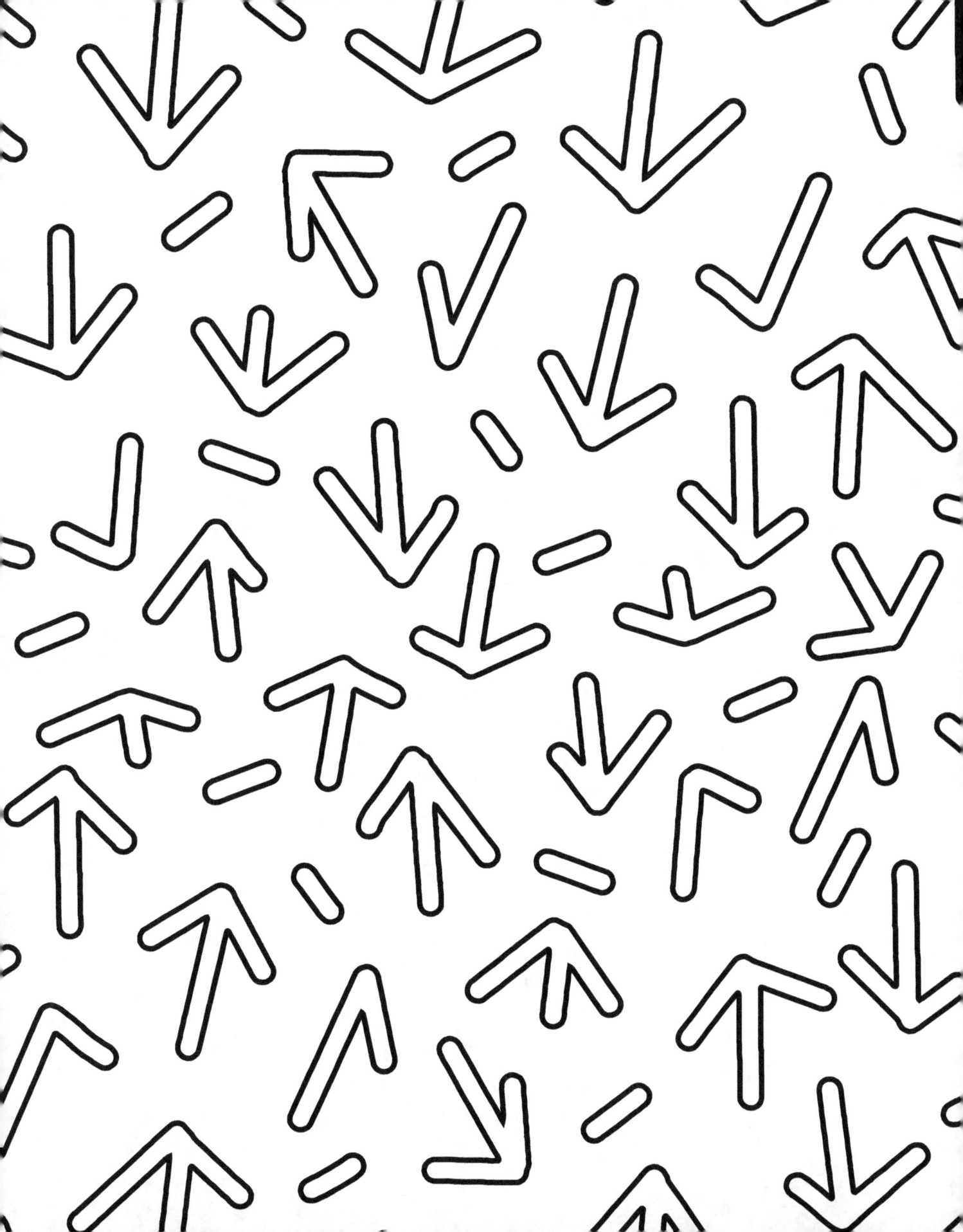

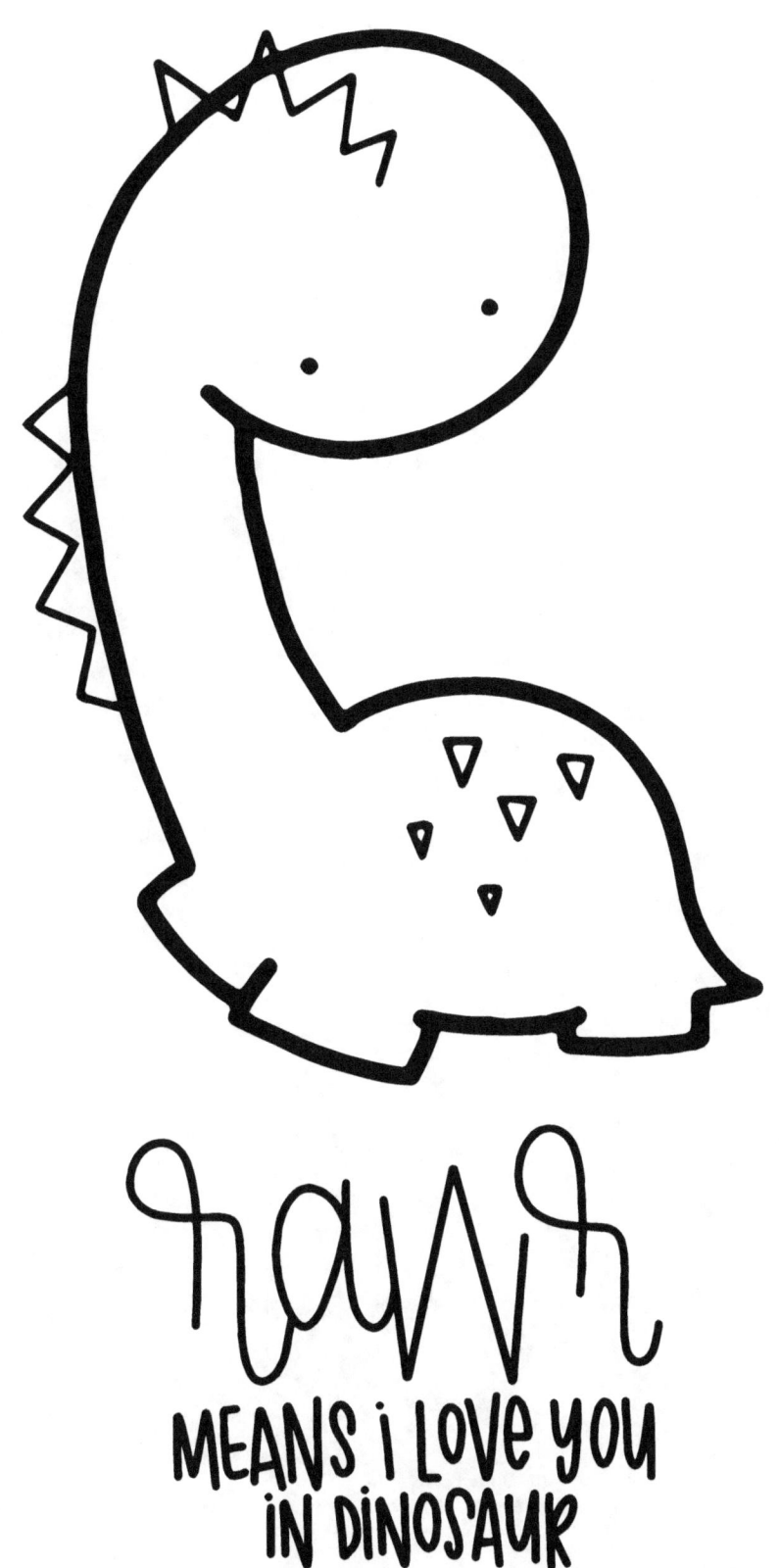

MEANS I LOVE YOU
IN DINOSAUR

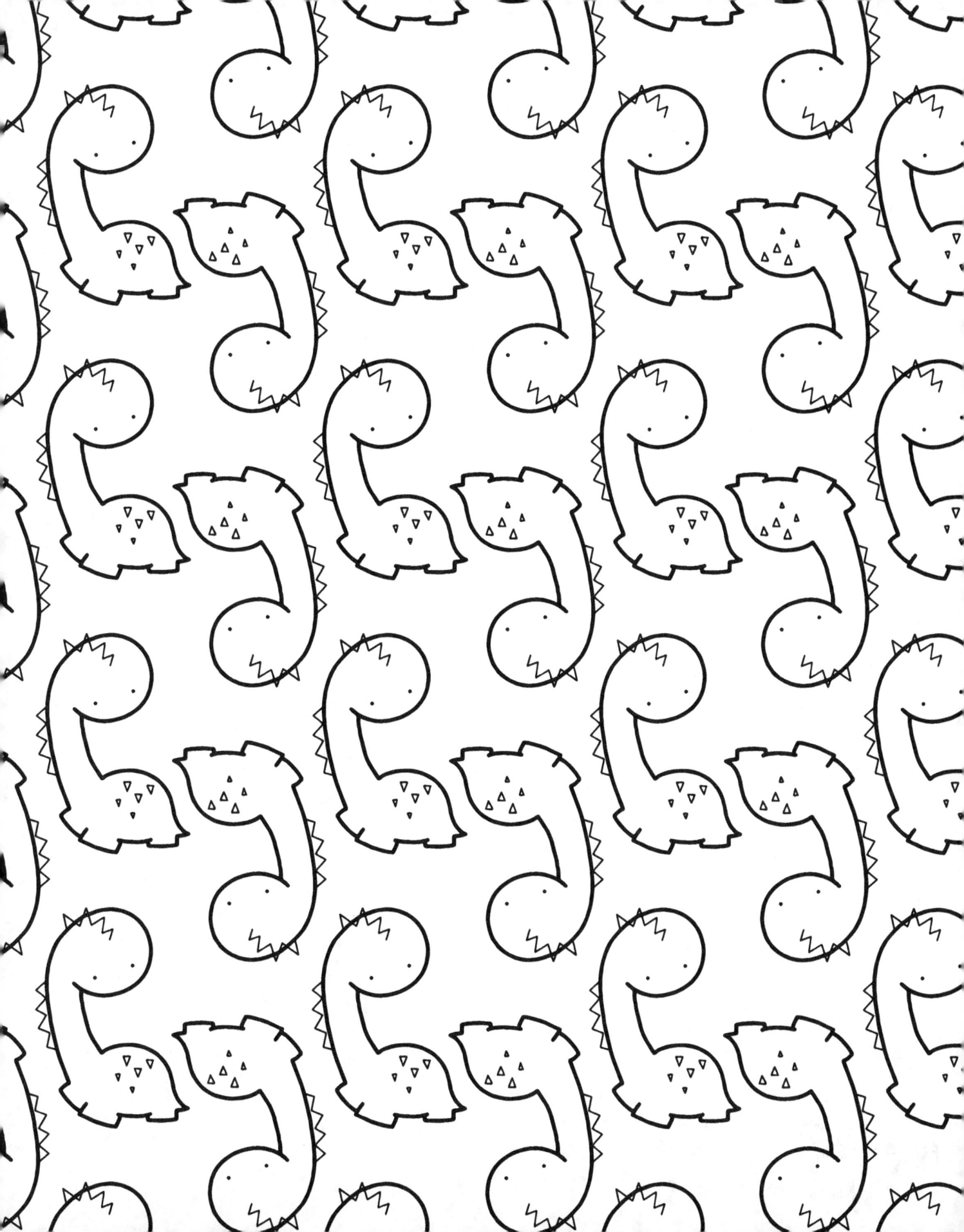